Milk Bread Cookbook for Beginners

100+ SUPER SOFT MILK BREAD RECIPES | A COMPREHENSIVE GUIDE TO MAKING HOMEMADE LOAVES WITH TANGZHONG AND YUDANE METHODS + BONUS MILK BREAD RECIPES FROM AROUND THE WORLD

Table of Contents

INTRODUCTION

Getting started with the best recipe for the famous Asian milk bread requires adequate and constant practice in milk bread making. First-time learners in cooking new recipes encounter numerous failures before getting a perfectly soft and buttery product. This is the main reason for coming up with this interesting cookbook to give you a variety of recipes to try out and find out which one best suits you.

For starters, milk bread is an enriched bread, which relies on fats to give the loaf its soft texture. Due to its origin, it is often referred to as "Hokkaidō milk bread" or "Japanese milk bread" in English. Among the Japanese, it is called shokupan – a regular loaf of bread that can be sliced and eaten. However, the exact origins of the bread are unknown, but some anthropologists have studied it widely and pointed out its development to Japan around the 20th century.

ASIAN BAKING HISTORY

Milk bread has been with us for several centuries now. Its invention can be traced to British baker Robert Clarke. Studies by Annie Sheng, an anthropologist at Cornell University on Asian bread, indicate that he opened Yokohama Bakery in Japan in 1862. However, even from her perspective, it is hard to conclude when milk bread, commonly known as shokupan in Japan, officially came into being. It generally refers to a loaf you cut, slice, and toast into sandwiches. A feathery center and a lightly sweet, milky flavor characterize it. This forms the basis through which various recipes originate.

Some milk bread is made with sandy flour and water paste (Yudane), while others are made of warmed milk and flour slurry, a Chinese equivalent of tangzhong. This gives the loaf the right bounce and longer shelf life. Some are just a mix of flour, water or milk, active dry yeast, salt, sugar, or on some occasions, butter. In Japan, some loaves, such as kakushoku, are shaped like a flat-topped Pullman, while others like yamata are rippled with rounded ridges. Others are twisted like a corkscrew before being baked. The most common shapes are the boxy, rectangular loaf (kakushoku) and the domed loaf (Yamagata shokupan). The method used and shape may differ, but that combination of flour, liquid, sugar, salt, and yeast leads to soft, fluffy crumbs (shokupan).

MILK BREAD METHODS

In Japanese, Yudane, and tangzhong are used interchangeably since they involve water roux; a gelatinous paste is composed of a heated mixture of flour and water used in bread making. Although they refer to the same thing, i.e., water roux, the method by which they are prepared is slightly different. Tangzhong method involves directly cooking the flour over heating with water, while the Yudane process involves "scalding" the flour with hot boiling water; there is no direct heating. A bread resulting from Yudane bread is soft with high moisture content and elasticity. In the scalding process, combined flour is set aside for at least 6 hours or overnight to create a gelatinized dough, while in tangzhong, once the dough is done, it can be used immediately after cooking and cooling.

TANGZHONG METHOD

In recent years, Asian bread's popularity has been due to a demand for the novelty flavors they sell. A big part of the ever-increasing fondness for these loaves of bread, they have a different mouth feel than classic bread. This cannot be compared to the meaty texture of supermarket bread and its delicate and chewy bite.

Many bread recipes from Asia utilize "tangzhong", or "water roux" techniques to achieve this special bread texture. Tangzhong technique originated from Japan involves cooking a mixture of flour and water to produce a slurry that will be added to the bread dough. The slurry typically has a combination of equal parts of flour and water used in thickening soups. Through precooking some of the flour, the gluten in the flour can stretch and develop. This gives it longer and more elastic strands. In bread, adding tangzhong slurry increases the amount of water the final bread dough can absorb. This provides the bread with the final softer texture since it is harder to dry out the dough during the baking process.

YUDANE METHOD

The Yudane method also has its roots in Japan. It became a widespread and popular way to bake bread in Asian countries. In her bread-making book called "Bread Doctor," Yvonne Chen has introduced the term "tangzhong" roux as a secret ingredient towards baking the super soft and light Japanese milk bread.

Tangzhoung and Yudane are often used synonymously, although they are different. "Hokkaido Milk Bread" or "Japanese Milk Bread" are made using the same principle, adding Yudane or Tangzhong roux to bread dough. Yudane uses a ratio of flour and water of 1:1, whereas "Tangzhong roux" is made by a 1:5 ratio of bread flour to water. This mixture is made by heating up to 65°C, cooling down to room temperature, and adding to the bread dough.

It is beneficial to trap more water in the dough. This allows the yeast to become more activated. Most commercial yeasts purchased are dried active yeast. Therefore, it is recommended to "soak" the yeast in a bit of warm water to reactivate it from its dormant state. Likewise, incorporating more water into the dough gives you an extra chance to activate the yeast. This applies to the yeast that may not have been woken up during the soaking stage.

To stay healthy, a proper diet is paramount. To achieve living quality and healthy life, one needs to access homemade sources of carbohydrates. Among other foods, milk bread is one of the cheapest sources available and easy to bake. Through homemade baking, you can save money, which may otherwise be spent on already processed bread. This cookbook gives the best guide on healthy living and provides amazing recipes to explore different cuisines of milk bread which do not necessarily originate from Japan.

The recipes provided are easy to follow stepwise, thus enabling one to enjoy their own homemade healthy meal. They are also well balanced and adhere to the dietitian requirements with limited sodium, potassium, carbohydrates, fats, and even calcium, contributing to lifestyle diseases. They also contain information on recipes, calories, protein, total fat, cholesterol, carbohydrate, fiber, and phosphorus content which can help vegetarians or those on a diet choose wisely what to cook. This has a more significant impact in aiding the body from developing other predisposing factors such as obesity, hypertension, and cardiovascular disease.

This cookbook provides a wide range of milk bread recipes that can be prepared easily at your comfort. This makes it a practical guide to enjoying different recipes from the culture within or without your country of origin. The recipes included are breakfast, snacks, and lunches, among others. Each recipe contains information on the ingredients required, the number of servings, and directions for meal preparation, preparation time, and cooking or baking. It also provides the serving size per person and Nutrition Facts per serving size, slice, and roll. This cookbook also provides suggestions on enjoying their milk bread and what other meals can accompany it. For other special dietary requirements, one should seek advice from their dietitian on their daily meal plans

1. SWEET MILK BREAD

Preparation time: 20 minutes

Cook time: 20 minutes

Resting time: 1 hour 30 minutes

Total time: 2 hours 10 minutes

Ingredients

- 1 cup of sugar
- 6 cups bread flour
- ½ teaspoon vinegar
- 1 teaspoon salt
- 3 tablespoons butter
- 2 tablespoons yeast
- 1 cup water
- 1 cup milk
- 2 eggs

Preparation

1. Dissolve sugar and yeast in warm water for 5 minutes or until it becomes frothy. Add the flour, salt, and sugar to a bowl and mix well.

2. At the center of the flour mixture, create a well. Add the yeast mixture, melted butter, eggs, milk, and vinegar. Begin to mix with your hands to form a sticky dough.
3. Transfer your dough to a floured work surface, and then knead. Dust the table with some flour, a little at a time, preventing the dough from sticking to the work surface.
4. After 10 minutes, transfer the dough inside the large mixing bowl. The dough should become smooth and elastic.
5. Coat it with a bit of oil. Cover with a damp cloth oil to prevent it from drying out. Place in a warmer place to rise for an hour or until it doubles in size.
6. After an hour, bring out your dough and punch it down; this removes the excess air. Do not overbeat it.
7. Transfer your dough back to the work surface. Divide it into four equal parts, and shape each into a loaf.
8. Grease the four loaf pans with oil. Dust them with flour, or you can spray them with a non-stick cooking spray.
9. Place the shaped dough inside the prepared loaf pans and cover them. Leave your dough to rise for approximately half an hour.
10. Once done, place the loaves inside a 350°F preheated oven. Bake for 20-25 minutes.
11. Leave to cool. Enjoy!

Nutrition Facts

Carbohydrates: 196g

Calories: 1026 kcal

Protein: 24g

Cholesterol: 110mg

Fat: 14g

Calcium: 112mg

Sodium: 722mg

Fiber: 5g

Iron: 9.1mg

2. CONDENSED MILK BREAD

Preparation time: 20 minutes

Cook time: 20 minutes

Total: 2 hours 10 minutes

Ingredients

Bread

- 1 cup milk warmed (37-47°C)
- ¼ cup sweetened condensed milk
- 1 egg (room temperature)
- ¼ cup butter softened, not melted
- 3 teaspoons rapid rise yeast
- 3 ¼ cups all-purpose flour
- 1 teaspoon of salt
- 2 tablespoons white granulated sugar

For the glaze

- 1 tablespoon of sweetened, condensed milk
- 1 tablespoon butter, softened

Preparation

To make the bread

1. Whisk the egg, warmed milk, condensed milk, and yeast in a bowl.
2. Add the sifted flour, salt, and sugar, then mix.

Knead the dough:

a) Turn your dough onto the surface with a bit of flour. Knead for 10 minutes; the dough becomes smooth and elastic by hand.

b) If using a stand mixer fitted with a dough hook, knead for 8 minutes. Knead the dough and then add butter. Rub the butter, then knead lightly until combined and smooth the dough.

3. Cover the dough with plastic wrap. Leave to rise for about 45-60 minutes in a warm, draft-free area of your kitchen.
4. Punch it down after the dough rises and turn it out of the bowl onto a well-floured surface. Knead for a minute. Shape the dough to form a small rectangle with your hands.
5. Use a rolling pin to roll out the dough to about 30cm by 42cm.
6. Roll your dough into a log shape starting from the shorter side.
7. Pinch the edges closed to seal and roll the log gently (with your hands) to smooth out the sealed edge.
8. Cut the rolled-up dough and divide it into approximately eight pieces about 1.5 inches thick
9. Grease and line a large 30.5 x 11 x 9.5 cm loaf pan with baking paper. Place the pieces into the preferred pan.
10. Allow the cut pieces to rise for 45 minutes; this allows the yeast more time to work to produce a lighter, chewier texture and fantastic flavor.
11. Brush with an egg and milk mixture to create a shiny and golden color of the crust
12. Preheat the oven to about 180°C or 160°C for a fan oven. Bake for about 25 minutes; the dough turns golden brown.

To make the glaze:

1. While your bread is still in the oven, prepare the glaze. Combine the condensed milk and melted butter in a small bowl and set aside.

2. Remove it from the oven. Turn out your bread from the baking tin. Brush with the prepared glaze and allow the glaze to dry. Slice the bread.

Nutrition Facts

Calories: 329 kcal

Carbohydrates: 49g

Protein: 9g

Fat: 11g

Cholesterol: 49mg

Sodium: 393mg

Potassium: 161mg

Fiber: 2g

3. SHOKUPAN

Preparation time: 2 hours

Cook time: 30 minutes

Yudane resting time: 8 hours

Total time: 2 hours 30 minutes

Ingredients

Yudane

- 40 ml boiling water above 90°
- 50g of Bread flour

Bread

- 200g Bread flour
- 150 ml milk at room temperature
- 15g sugar
- 10g unsalted butter (room temperature)
- 3g each dry instant yeast
- 5g salt

Preparation

Make the Yudane the night before.

1. Place bread flour in a bowl. Add boiling water and mix well. Put cling wrap. Refrigerate overnight.
2. Pour milk into a stand mixer bowl. Add yeast, butter, and sugar to the bowl. Add the Yudane as you tear the dough into small pieces. Add the flour, bread, and salt.
3. Combine all ingredients on low speed 1 after attaching the kneading hook onto the stand mixer.
4. Once you combine all ingredients, turn the speed to 5 or 6. Knead the dough for 20 minutes.
5. Roll the dough round. Place it into an oiled bowl and wrap with cling wrap to rise for about 45 min to an hour at about 30°C; it will double the size.
6. Test if the dough has risen by poking the dough using a dusted finger. If it does not bounce back and the hole you poked stays there, it is ready.
7. Cut it into two equal parts with a scraper and then roll them.
8. Cover the rolled dough with a wet cloth. Stand it for 20 minutes bench time. Roll out each dough into a 15 x 20 cm rectangle with a rolling pin.
9. Fold the dough tightly. Do not let any air in towards the center from left and right. Rotate the dough 90 degrees. Roll it from one end.
10. Spray one loaf bread tin lightly. Place the rolled dough at the end of the tin facing the center.
11. Cover it with a wet cloth. Let it rise again until the dough rises to the size of the bread in about 30 minutes.
12. Start to preheat the oven to 185°C. Bake the dough for about 30 minutes in preheated oven.
13. Remove the bread from the tin. Cool it down on a rack.
14. Whisk an egg, lightly brush over the bread dough.

Nutrition Facts

Calories: 1112 kcal

Carbohydrates: 200g

Sodium: 2396mg

Protein: 34g

Fat: 17g

Cholesterol: 36mg

Fiber: 6g

Calcium: 199mg

4. ORANGE CHEESECAKE BREAKFAST ROLLS

Prep: 50 min

Rising Bake: 25 min

Ingredients

- 8 cups all-purpose flour

- ¾ cup warm water (110°C to 115°C)

- 3 tablespoons butter, melted

- 1 cup sugar

- 2 large eggs, room temperature

- 1 ¾ cups warm 2% milk (110°C to 115°C)

- 2 -(1/4 ounce each) active dry yeast

- 1 ½ teaspoons salt

Filling

- 1 package (8 ounces) cream cheese, softened

- 1/2 cup sugar

- 1 tablespoon thawed orange juice concentrate

- 1/2 teaspoon vanilla extract

Glaze

- 2 cups confectioners' sugar

- 3 tablespoons orange juice

- 1 teaspoon grated orange zest

Preparation

1. Dissolve your dry yeast in warm water in a large bowl. Add 5 cups flour, eggs, milk, butter, sugar, and salt. Stir in enough remaining flour to form a firm dough.

2. For about 6-8 minutes, knead until smooth and elastic dough on a floured surface. Place it in a greased bowl and turn once to grease the top. Cover your dough and let it rise in a warm place; it will double in about 1 hour.

3. Beat sugar, cream cheese, orange juice, concentrate, and vanilla until smooth in a small bowl. Punch your dough down, turn onto a lightly floured surface, and divide it in half. Roll one portion into an 18x7-inch rectangle, and then spread half the filling to within 1/2 inch of its edges.

4. Starting with the long side, roll it up jelly-roll style—Pinch seam to seal, cut it into twelve slices, and place the cut side down in a greased 13x9-inch baking pan. Repeat with remaining dough and filling. Cover the dough. Let rise for about half an hour.

5. Preheat oven to 350°C. Bake rolls for 30 minutes or until golden brown. Combine confectioners' sugar, orange juice, and zest and drizzle over warm rolls. Refrigerate.

Nutrition Facts

Calories: 284

Fat: 6g

Cholesterol: 33mg

Sodium: 201mg

Carbohydrates: 52g

Protein: 32

5. KOREAN GARLIC CHEESE BREAD

Preparation time: 20 minutes

Cook time: 40 minutes

Resting time: 2 hours

Total Time: 3 hours

Ingredients

- 1 lb. bread flour
- 2 tablespoons instant yeast
- 1 cup milk
- 1 tablespoon salt
- 3 eggs
- 1 cup sugar
- 1 cup unsalted butter
- ¼ cup garlic, minced
- 5 tablespoons condensed milk
- 1 tablespoon fresh parsley
- 2 cups cream cheese
- ½ cup powdered milk
- 5 tablespoons water

Preparation

For the bread

1. Combine the yeast, 60 grams of sugar, and milk in a bowl. Mix well until the sugar and yeast dissolve. Add the flour, salt, and two eggs to the mixture. Fold the ingredients together; there will be no more flour pockets seen.
2. Place your dough on your work surface. Knead it for a minute. Add in 40 grams of unsalted butter and fold it in the dough.
3. Knead for another 8 minutes. Form it into a round shape and put it in a large bowl. Cover it with cling wrap and let it rest for about 2 hours; the dough will be doubled in size. After resting, knead the dough for over 5 minutes to release the air inside and even it out.
4. Divide your dough into 16 even pieces. Shape it into buns and let the dough rest again for 30 minutes.
5. Bake your dough in an oven at about 180°C for 20 minutes. The bread will turn to a dark golden brown. Let it cool for 60 minutes

Cream cheese filling

1. In a bowl, mix the water and powdered milk. Set the bowl aside and then grab another bowl. Add your cream cheese and 30 grams of sugar and stir it well.
2. Mix your powdered milk mixture to the cream cheese mixture. Stir well; this will ensure there are no more lumps.
3. Put it in a piping bag. Place it in the refrigerator.
4. For the garlic sauce:
5. Mix 160 grams of unsalted butter (melted), one egg, minced garlic, condensed milk, 25 grams of sugar, and parsley in a bowl.

To combine

1. Cut the bread into four or six segments, but ensure it is not all the way through. Pipe the cream cheese filling into the gaps. Add a generous amount of garlic sauce to the bread.
2. Bake for 10 minutes.
3. Remove from oven and serve warm.

Nutrition Facts

Calories: 432

Fat: 27g

Carbs: 37g

Fiber: 0g

Sugar: 15g

Protein: 9g

6. SOFT AND FLUFFY JAPANESE MILK BREAD

Prep time: 1 hours 5 mins

Cook time: 25 mins

Total time: 1 hour 30 mins

Equipment

- Kitchen scale
- 1 lb. loaf pan

Ingredients

- 432g milk
- 24g butter
- 12g sea salt
- 30g sugar
- 600g bread flour
- 9.6g active dry yeast
- 6g dough enhancer

Preparation

1. Attach the dough hook to the stand mixer and add all the ingredients except the butter. Mix the dough at low speed until there is no more dry flour. Add the butter. Beat on high speed. Form your dough into a ball once it is ready; smooth and glossy surface. Check for proper gluten development using the windowpane test for around 13 minutes.
2. Form a smooth round ball. Place the dough into a see-through proofing container that has been coated with oil; allow it to rise in a warm, humid environment.
3. On a well-floured surface, place your dough and then divide it into six even pieces. Roll each into a ball and loosely cover. Let it rest for 15 minutes.

4. Roll each ball into an oval shape. Then, flip it over so the surface (crust) is on the bottom, and do a letter fold (2- folds). Roll it to form a spiral shape and pinch the seam closed. Proceed to place three spirals in each 1 lb. loaf pan. Repeat for the other pieces.
5. Proof in a warm, humid place; it will double in size
6. Preheat the oven to 356° F. Bake at 356° F for about 25 minutes; the crust will be golden brown. Immediately remove from the oven, brush on an egg wash coating for a shiny crust. The heat from the bread will cook the egg, giving the bread a shiny golden crust.

Nutrition Facts

Calories: 222 kcal

Carbohydrates: 41g

Protein: 8g

Fat: 3g

Cholesterol: 6mg

Sodium: 419mg

Potassium: 112mg

Fiber: 1g

Sugar: 5g

Calcium: 53mg

Iron: 1mg

7. SAVOURY WOOL ROLL BREAD

Prep: 30 mins

Cook: 45 mins

Additional: 2 hours 40 mins

Total: 3 hours 55 mins

Equipment

- 18 cm round cake form

Ingredients

Tangzhong/water roux

- 20g bread flour
- 120 ml water

Yeast mix

- 2g sugar
- 75 ml water
- 5g active dry yeast

Main dough

- 300g bread flour
- 50g of egg (leave the rest of the egg as egg wash)
- 14g sugar
- 6g salt
- 5g condensed milk
- 25g butter (to grease the baking form)
- Egg wash

Fillings (optional)

- Green onion
- Salt
- White pepper

Preparation

Tangzhong

1. Combine the flour and water in a small pot and put it on medium heat; keep mixing until it becomes a paste. Set aside to cool down before use.

Yeast mix

1. Add sugar and water to a bowl. Mix it over a water bath until it is between 45-50°C. Add the yeast and stir it. Leave it aside to dissolve for 5 minutes.

Main dough

2. Add sugar, flour, salt, condensed milk, egg, tangzhong/water roux, and yeast mix in a large mixing bowl.
3. Knead by hand or a mixer with a dough hook for about 4 minutes. Starting with a hand mixer with the dough hook on the slowest mode, increase the speed a level up to mix for another 10 minutes; knead it until a smooth dough forms.
4. Add the butter to the dough and knead again for 10 minutes; a smooth dough is formed.
5. Cover your dough and leave it in a warm place to proof for 45 mins; it will double in size.
6. At the same time, chop the green onion into small pieces and set them aside. Brush a layer of butter in the cake form

7. After the first rising, press out all the air and put it on a floured surface. Divide the dough into five pieces. Shape each dough into a small round ball. Cover with a cling film and leave it to rest for about 10 minutes.
8. Take out one of the dough balls, flatten it with a rolling pin to form an oval shape, and cut it into stripes for half of the oval shape. Add the green onion, white pepper, and a pinch of salt on the other side.
9. On the green onion side, fold the two outer edges of your dough towards the middle. Start rolling it from the green onion side to the side with the stripes.
10. Repeat for all five dough balls and put the product in the cake form - on edge like a ring.
11. Cover cake form and place it in a warm place to rise again for around 30 mins.
12. Preheat the oven to 175°C. Brush some egg wash or milk on top. Bake in the oven for 18 mins and then remove from the cake form to cool down.

Nutrition Facts

Calories: 221.8

Protein: 5.4g

Carbohydrates: 36.7g

Fat: 6.4g

Cholesterol: 26.2mg

Calcium: 29.5mg

Iron: 2.1mg

Magnesium: 21mg

Potassium: 115mg

Sodium: 159.8mg

8. JAPANESE TARO MILK BREAD

Prep time: 1 hour

Cook time: 45 minutes

Additional time: 10 hours

Total time: 11 hours 45 minutes

Ingredients

- 250g bread flour

- 160g milk
- 25g granulated sugar
- 20g condensed milk
- 3g of salt
- 3g active dry yeast
- 20g unsalted butter
- 8g taro powder

Yudane

- 15g boiling water
- 15g bread flour

Preparation

Make Yudane 8 hours ahead

1. Add boiling water and bread flour in a small bowl and mix well with a spatula. Let it cool down, and then keep it in the refrigerator for 8 hours with plastic wrap covered.

Main dough

1. Add all ingredients except butter in a large mixing bowl and combine well. Transfer the dough to a flat surface and knead it until smooth for 10 minutes; at this point, your dough will be super sticky.
2. Add butter into the dough, keep kneading it for another 10- 20 minutes and allow resting for 10 minutes, allowing the dough to produce more gluten so that it would not be too sticky afterward.
3. Throw the dough on the flat surface, and then lift it. Repeat the technique 50 times. Knead the dough for 5 minutes; this smoothens the dough quickly.
4. After kneading, use plastic wrap to cover your dough in a bowl. Let it rise for 1 hour
5. After the first fermentation and the dough has doubled in size, poke a hole in the middle of the dough to check if it is ready. If the hole does not go back, which means the dough has been raised appropriately.
6. Transfer the dough to a flat surface, press the dough to release the air, and then knead it to a ball shape.
7. Knead it to a ball shape and divide it into three equal pieces. Add 2g taro powder to one of the doughs and 6g taro powder to another. Knead the dough until the color is combined.
8. Knead three doughs and roll them into a ball shape. Let them rest for 15 minutes with plastic wrap covered.
9. Shape and roll all three doughs into strips of the same length.
10. Braid the three doughs together.
11. Transfer it to a loaf pan, and let it rise for 1 hour with the plastic wrap covered.
12. Preheat your oven to 350 F and bake for 35 minutes.

Nutrition Facts

Calories: 1355 cal

Total Fat: 24g

Saturated Fat: 13.8g

Cholesterol: 63mg

Sodium: 1386mg

Carbohydrates: 247.1g

Fiber: 7.8g

Protein: 35.5g

9. UBE MARBLE BREAD

Prep Time: 20 mins

Cook Time: 35 mins

Resting Time: 1 hr. 45 mins

Total Time: 2 hours 40 mins

Ingredients

- 250g all-purpose flour or bread flour
- 1 batch Matcha Shokupan
- 85 ml whole milk warm
- 6g active dry yeast
- 15g granulated sugar
- 100g ube purple yam puree
- 1 large egg
- 1 tablespoon purple yam or purple sweet potato powder
- 15g unsalted butter

Preparation

For ube purple yam dough

1. Combine active dry yeast, the warmed milk, and sugar in a small bowl. Stir it and set it aside to let the yeast activate.
2. Add in flour, ube purple yam puree, ube powder/purple yam, and egg in a stand mixer bowl fitted with a dough hook,
3. Add the yeast mixture into the flour. Knead until it comes together, and then add in the butter. Continue kneading until the dough is smooth and shiny.
4. Transfer your dough to a lightly oiled bowl, cover, and let it rest in a warm location until doubled in bulk.

Assembling & baking

1. Once your dough has risen, deflate it and divide it in half. Take the risen plain dough and divide that into half as well.
2. Cut each dough into pieces and roll it into balls. Place the dough balls in a loaf pan randomly, with plain dough alternating with the purple use yam dough.
3. Repeat it with the second half in another loaf pan, and then cover it with a plastic wrap or a damp cloth. Let it rise in a warm location.
4. Preheat oven to 350°F and bake for 35 minutes, or until a thermometer-inserted registers 190F.
5. Remove from oven and transfer to a wire rack. Let the bread completely cool before slicing.

Nutrition Facts

Calories: 55kcal

Carbohydrates: 10g

Protein: 2g

Fat: 1g

Cholesterol: 9mg

Potassium: 55mg

Fiber: 1g

Calcium: 8mg

Iron: 1mg

10. UBE SWIRL MILK BREAD

Prep Time: 3 hours

Cook Time: 30 mins

Total Time: 3 hours 30 mins

Ingredients

Tangzhong

- 100 ml water at room temperature
- 20g bread flour

Dough

- 5g instant yeast
- 290g bread flour
- 25g unsalted butter (room temperature)
- 6g salt
- 5g milk powder
- 30g sugar
- 130 ml of milk
- 1 large egg at room temperature

Ube coloring paste

- 1 tablespoon Suncore Foods Purple Sweet Potato Powder
- 1 teaspoon Ube Extract
- 1 tablespoon of water

Egg wash

- 1 tablespoon milk
- 1 large egg

Preparation

Tangzhong making

1. Pour flour and water in a small saucepan and whisk until no lumps are left. Heat over medium heat while constantly whisking; the mixture will thicken into a paste. Let it cool in a bowl to room temperature and leave for 1 hour before using.

Ube Paste Making

1. Mix the purple sweet potato powder, ube flavoring, and water until it forms a paste. Set aside.
2. Combine the flour, yeast, milk powder, sugar, and salt in a stand mixer with the hook attachment. Add tangzhong, warmed milk, and egg. Knead on low speed until ingredients are combined for about 7 minutes.
3. When the dough has formed, add the softened butter and increase the speed. Knead it until they combine for about 7 minutes; the dough should be tacky but not sticky.
4. Divide the dough into two equal parts. Set aside one-half of the dough.
5. Place your second dough back in the mixer and add the ube paste. Knead until it combines. Shape your dough, place in two lightly greased bowls, and let it proof in a warm place for about 1-2 hours; it will double, and then remove it from the bowl.
6. Roll out your white dough into an 8.5 x 12-inch rectangle on a lightly floured surface; the dough should be thin. Roll out the ube dough into the same size as the white dough and place it on top of the white dough; roll out the dough to merge.
7. Carefully roll the dough down the longer 12-inch side of the dough and pitch it at the end to seal the seam.
8. Place your logs seam side down in an 8.5 x 4.5 loaf pan and then proof in a warm place for another 30 min to 1 hour until doubled in size.
9. Preheat oven to 355°C and brush with egg wash. Bake for 30 minutes.

Nutrition Facts

Calories: 1670kcal

Carbohydrates: 266g

Protein: 56g

Fat: 40g

Cholesterol: 400mg

Sodium: 2549mg

Potassium: 744mg

Fiber: 9g

Sugar: 40g

11. AMISH MILK BREAD

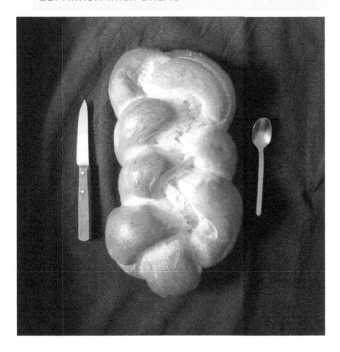

Prep: 30 mins

Cook: 40 mins

Rise: 105 mins

Total: 2 hours 55 mins

Ingredients

- 6 cups bread flour, divided
- 2 ¼ -ounce packets dry active yeast
- ¼ cup water, warm
- 2 cups milk, room temperature
- 1 teaspoon salt
- 2 tablespoons butter, soft
- 1 tablespoon brown sugar, packed
- 1 teaspoon vegetable oil

Preparation

1. In a large bowl, gently stir together warm water and the yeast. Add brown sugar, salt, milk, and butter, and then stir well to incorporate. Add four cups of flour. Mix well and add enough of the remaining flour to make a dough that follows the spoon around the bowl.

2. Proceed by turning the dough out onto a lightly floured surface. Knead for 10 minutes. Add more flour as needed; the dough will be firm and smooth to the touch.
3. Grease a bowl with vegetable oil. Place your dough, turning it over to lightly grease the top. Cover with a clean cloth. Let rise in a draft-free place for an hour.
4. After an hour, firmly punch down the dough. Proceed by turning the dough out onto a lightly floured board. Knead for 5 minutes; bubbles will move out of the bread.
5. Divide dough into two equal portions. Shape each dough half into a loaf.
6. Place each piece of the loaf into a greased 9 x 5-inch bread pan. Cover and then let rise in a warm, draft-free place for 45 minutes; it will double in size.
7. Preheat the oven to about 350 F. Bake the loaves for 40 minutes; the top will be golden brown, and the bread sounds hollow when tapped.
8. Remove the loaves from the pans and allow them to cool down on a rack.
9. Serve and enjoy!

Nutrition Facts

Calories: 175 cal

Total fat: 2g

Saturated fat: 1g

Cholesterol: 4mg

Sodium: 127mg

Total carbohydrate: 32g

Protein: 6g

12. CONDENSED MILK BREAD ROLLS

Prep Time: 15 mins

Cook Time: 30 mins

Proofing Time: 3 hours

Total Time: 3 hours 45 mins

Ingredients

Dough

- 3 1/4 cups all-purpose flour
- 1 tablespoon instant yeast

- 1/2 teaspoon salt
- 1 cup milk room temperature
- 1/2 cup condensed milk
- 1 egg large
- 2 oz. butter room temperature, cubed
- For the egg wash
- 1 Egg
- 1 tablespoon milk

Glaze

- 3 tablespoons condensed milk
- 1 tablespoon butter (room temperature)

Preparation

1. Sift the flour through a fine sieve mesh into a mixing bowl and add the rest of the dry ingredients.
2. While using a dough hook, add milk, condensed milk, and egg to the dry mixture at slow speed. Mix them until the cohesive dough starts to form about a minute. Scrape with a rubber spatula if necessary.
3. Increase speed to medium from low, then add butter, one piece at a time, and mix until butter is fully incorporated. Keep mixing the dough until it is smooth and elastic, about 2 minutes. Make sure no dry flour remains on the bottom of the mixing bowl. Don't add more flour to the mixture, even if the dough is slightly wet.
4. Transfer the dough to a lightly greased mixing bowl while using your hand to knead your dough a few times to form a smooth round dough
5. Turn the smooth dough seam side down; cover the bowl tightly with plastic wrap, and let the dough rise until it doubles in about 1.5 to 2 hours. Do not rush this proofing process, or you will end up with heavy, not fluffy rolls
6. In the meantime, grease your baking pan, then punch down the dough and carefully transfer it to a lightly floured counter when the dough is ready. Divide the dough into eight equal pieces.
7. Work with each piece of dough at a time. Remember to cover the rest with plastic wrap if you sometimes need to form each small dough. Stretch your dough by using your fingers and pinch the edges together at the bottom to create a smooth dough
8. Place your dough seam side down back on the counter. Drag it in a small circle to create a smooth round ball using your hand. Transfer the ball, seam side down, to an already greased baking pan. Repeat it for the remaining pieces.
9. Arrange the balls in your pan and lightly cover them with plastic wrap. Let them rise until they almost double in size. Make sure that they don't rise above the rim of the pan
10. Preheat oven to 350F. Gently brush dinner rolls with egg wash mixture, bake from 25 to 30 minutes, and rotate the pan halfway. The dinner rolls should have a deep or bright golden-brown crust, depending on your preferences.
11. When the rolls are done baking, take them out and allow them to cool down for 7 minutes at room temperature. Lightly brush the rolls with a layer of condensed milk glaze on top while still warm. Let the rolls cool for about 30 minutes to 60 minutes
12. Serve

Nutrition Facts

Calories: 371

Fat: 12g

Cholesterol: 72mg

Sodium: 273mg

Potassium: 218mg

Carbohydrates: 55g

Fiber: 2g

Sugar: 16g

Protein: 10g

Calcium: 128mg

Iron: 3mg

13. CINNAMON SWIRL BREAD

Prep: 25 min

Rising bake: 30 min

Ingredients

- 2 (1/4 ounce each) active dry yeast
- 1/3 cup warm water (110° to 115°)
- 1 cup warm 2% milk (110° to 115°)
- 1 cup sugar, divided
- 2 large eggs, room temperature
- 6 tablespoons butter, softened
- 1 ½ teaspoons salt
- 6 cups all-purpose flour
- 2 tablespoons ground cinnamon

Preparation

1. In a large bowl, dissolve yeast in warm water. Add milk, 1/2 cup sugar, eggs, butter, salt, and 3 cups flour; beat on medium speed until smooth. Stir in enough remaining flour to form a soft dough.
2. Turn dough onto a floured surface; knead until smooth and elastic, 6-8 minutes. Place in a greased bowl, turning once to grease the top. Cover and let it rise for about 1 hour in a warm place until it doubles.

3. Mix cinnamon and remaining sugar. Punch it down; turn onto a lightly floured surface. Divide in half and roll each portion into an 18x8-inch rectangle; sprinkle each with about 1/4 cup cinnamon sugar within 1/2 in. of edges. Roll up jelly-roll style, starting with a short side; pinch seam to seal—place in 2 greased 9x5-inch loaf pans, seam side down.
4. Cover with kitchen towels; let rise for about 1 ½ hours in a warm place until it doubles.
5. Preheat oven to 350°C and bake for about 30-35 minutes until golden brown. Remove it from pans to wire racks to cool.

Nutrition Facts

Calories: 132

Fat: 3g

Cholesterol: 20mg

Sodium: 141mg

Carbohydrate: 23g

Protein: 3g

14. SWEDISH RYE BREAD

Prep: 25 min

Rising Bake: 30 min

Ingredients

- 1/4-ounce active dry yeast
- 1 ¾ cups warm water (at 110° to 115°C), divided
- 1/4 cup packed brown sugar
- 1/4 cup molasses
- 2 tablespoons shortening
- 2 teaspoons salt
- 2 ½ cups rye flour
- 4 ¼ cups all-purpose flour
- 2 tablespoons butter, melted

Preparation

1. In a bowl, dissolve yeast in 1/4 cup water. Add sugar, molasses, shortening, salt, and remaining water; stir well. Add rye flour; beat until smooth. Add enough all-purpose flour to form a soft dough.

2. Turn onto a floured surface; knead until smooth and elastic, 6-8 minutes. Place in a greased bowl, turning once to grease top. Cover and let rise in a warm place until doubled about 1-1/2 hours. Punch dough down.

3. Shape into 4 round loaves. Place on greased baking sheets. Cover and let rise until doubled, 45-60 minutes. Bake at 350° until golden brown, 30-35 minutes. Brush with butter.

Nutrition Facts

Calories: 109

Fat: 2g

Cholesterol: 2mg

Sodium: 155mg

Carbohydrate: 21g

Protein: 2g

15. BUTTERY BUBBLE BREAD

Prep: 25 min.

Rising Bake: 30 min

Ingredients

- 1/4-ounce active dry yeast
- 1 cup warm water (110° to 115°C)
- 1/2 cup sugar
- 1/2 cup shortening
- 1 large egg, room temperature
- 1/2 teaspoon salt
- 4 ½ cups all-purpose flour, divided
- 6 tablespoons butter, melted

Preparation

1. Dissolve yeast in warm water in a large bowl. Add an egg, sugar, shortening, salt, and 1 cup of flour, then beat until smooth. Stir in enough remaining flour to form a soft dough.

2. Turn onto a floured surface; knead until smooth and elastic, 6-8 minutes. Place in a greased bowl, turning once to grease top. Cover and let rise in a warm place until doubled, about 1 hour.

3. Punch dough down. Turn onto a lightly floured surface and shape into 1 ½ -inch balls. Dip the balls in butter and arrange evenly in a greased 9-in. fluted tube pan. Drizzle with remaining butter. Cover and let rise in a warm place until doubled, about 45 minutes.
4. Bake at 350° for 30-35 minutes or until golden brown. Cool for 5 minutes before inverting onto a serving platter. Serve warm.

Nutrition Facts

Calories: 237

Fat: 11g

Cholesterol: 25mg

Sodium: 122mg

Carbohydrate: 30g

Protein: 4g

16. LEMON BLUEBERRY BREAD

Prep: 15 min

Bake: 1 hour

Ingredients

- 1/3 cup butter, melted
- 1 cup sugar
- 3 tablespoons lemon juice
- 2 large eggs, room temperature
- 1-1/2 cups all-purpose flour
- 1 teaspoon baking powder
- 1/2 teaspoon salt
- 1/2 cup 2% milk
- 1 cup fresh or frozen blueberries
- 1/2 cup chopped nuts
- 2 tablespoons grated lemon zest

Glaze

- 2 tablespoons lemon juice
- 1/4 cup sugar

Preparation

1. Beat the butter, sugar, lemon juice, and eggs in a large bowl. Combine baking powder, flour, and salt and stir into egg mixture alternately with milk, beating well after each addition. Fold in the blueberries, nuts, and lemon zest.
2. Transfer to a greased 8x4-inch loaf pan. Bake for 60-70 minutes at 350°C or until a toothpick inserted in the center comes out clean. Cool for 10 minutes before removing from pan to a wire rack.
3. Combine glaze ingredients; drizzle over warm bread. Cool completely.

Nutrition Facts

Calories: 181

Fat: 7g

Cholesterol: 38mg

Sodium: 149mg

Carbohydrate: 27g

Protein: 3g

17. GRAPEFRUIT WALNUT BREAD

Prep: 20 min

Bake: 1 hour plus cooling

Ingredients

- 1 cup butter-flavored shortening
- 2 cups sugar
- 4 large eggs, room temperature
- 3 cups all-purpose flour
- 3 teaspoons baking powder
- 1 teaspoon salt
- 1 cup 2% milk
- 1 cup finely chopped walnuts
- 2 tablespoons grated grapefruit zest

Glaze

- 1/2 cup sugar
- 1/2 cup grapefruit juice

Preparation

1. Preheat oven to 350°. Grease and flour two 9x5-inch loaf pans.
2. Beat shortening and sugar until crumbly in a large bowl. Add an egg at a time, beating well after each addition. Whisk flour, salt, and baking powder in another bowl; add to creamed mixture alternately with milk, beat well after each addition. Fold in zest and walnuts.
3. Transfer to prepared pans. Bake for about 60 minutes until a toothpick inserted in the center comes out clean. Meanwhile, whisk glaze ingredients. Remove pans from the oven; immediately brush with glaze.
4. Cool in pan for 10 minutes before removing a wire rack to cool completely.

Nutrition Facts

Calories: 263

Fat: 12g

Cholesterol: 32mg

Sodium: 176mg

Carbohydrate: 35g

Protein: 4g

18. ONE-BOWL CHOCOLATE CHIP BREAD

Prep: 20 minutes

Bake: 65 minutes

Ingredients

- 3 large eggs, room temperature
- 1 cup sugar
- 2 cups sour cream
- 3 cups self-rising flour
- 2 cups semisweet chocolate chips

Preparation

1. Beat eggs, sour cream, and sugar until it is well blended. Gradually stir in flour. Fold in chocolate chips. Transfer to a greased 9x5-inch loaf pan.

2. Preheat oven to 350°C and bake for 65-75 minutes until a toothpick comes out clean. Cool it in a pan for 5 minutes before removing it to a wire rack to cool.

Nutrition Facts

Calories: 306

Fat: 13g

Cholesterol: 42mg

Sodium: 305mg

Carbohydrate: 44g

Protein: 5g

19. CARAWAY SEED RYE BREAD

Prep: 20 min

Rising Bake: 25 min

Ingredients

- 3 ¼ cups all-purpose flour, divided
- 1/4 cup packed brown sugar
- 2 cups warm water (110° to 115°C), divided
- 1 tablespoon caraway seeds
- 1 tablespoon canola oil
- 2 -(1/4 ounce each) active dry yeast
- 2 ½ cups rye flour
- 2 teaspoons salt

Preparation

1. In a large bowl, dissolve yeast in 1/2 cup warm water. Add brown sugar, caraway, oil, salt, and remaining water; mix well. Stir in rye flour and 1 cup all-purpose flour; beat until smooth. Add enough remaining all-purpose flour to form a soft dough.
2. Turn onto a floured surface; knead until smooth and elastic, 6-8 minutes. Place in a greased bowl, turning once to grease top. Cover and let rise in a warm place until doubled, about 1 hour.
3. Punch dough down; divide in half. Shape each half into a ball; place in 2 greased 8-in. round baking pans or ovenproof skillets. Flatten balls to a 6-in. diameter. Cover and let rise until nearly doubled, about 30 minutes. Bake at 375° for 25-30 minutes or until golden brown.

Nutrition Facts

Calories: 126

Fat: 1g

Sodium: 238mg

Carbohydrate: 26g

Protein: 3g

20. SOFT MILK BREAD ROLLS

Prep Time: 10 mins

Cook Time: 18 mins

Rise Time: 1 hours 45 mins

Total Time: 2 hours 13 mins

Ingredients

- 1 tbsp. milk to mix with the egg yolk
- 5 cups all-purpose flour
- 1 ¼ cup lukewarm milk
- 2 large eggs (lightly beaten)
- 2 tbsp. butter (room temperature)
- 2 tbsp. sugar plus 1 tsp.
- 1 ½ tsp. kosher salt
- 2 ¼ tsp. instant yeast
- 1 egg yolk mixed + one tablespoon of milk

Preparation

1. Warm the milk in the microwave and set it aside. Beat two eggs in another bowl and set them aside.
2. Sift five cups of all-purpose flour into a large standing mixing bowl using a sieve. Add the sugar, salt, and yeast and stir in the baking machine. While your machine is running, slowly add the milk. Add the beaten eggs and scrape the side of the bowl using a baking spatula; this will incorporate the flour. While you are mixing, add the butter. Set the timer to 12 minutes, increase the speed to 2. Knead until the machine timer goes off.
3. Lightly sprinkle flour to a clean surface area. Place the dough on the floured surface. Shape the dough into a ball.
4. Place the dough in a clean bowl clean; the bowl is lightly oiled to avoid sticking. Using a kitchen towel, cover the bowl. Let rise for 60 minutes in a warm location; the dough will double.
5. Flour a clean surface; punch a hole in the middle of the dough. Transfer the dough to the floured surface.
6. Lightly press down onto the dough and shape it into a 12" square diameter.
7. After lining a baking dish with parchment paper, pull out a small amount of dough, shape it into a ball. Roll it in a circular motion on a floured surface in a circular motion. Place it on the lined baking dish about ½ inch apart.
8. Repeat the steps for all the dough. Cover the dough with a clean towel. Let it rise; this is done in a warm environment. Once the dough has risen after 45 minutes, preheat the oven to 325 F. Whisk together the 1 tbsp of milk and egg yolk in a separate bowl.
9. Uncover the dough and lightly brush the dough's top with the egg mixture. Do not press them down while adding the mixture; this may prevent them from rising when baking.
10. Bake the bread for about 18 minutes in the oven at 325°C. Base with melted butter. Enjoy!

Nutrition Facts

Calories: 372.5kcal

Carbohydrates: 73.6g

Protein: 11.8g

Fat: 3.1g

Cholesterol: 6.1mg

Fiber: 3.2g

Calcium: 82.4mg

Iron: 3.9mg

21. MILK TOASTED SANDWICHES

Total Time: 15–30 minutes

Ingredients

- Six slices - large sized sandwiches bread
- 1 cup - milk
- 2 tbsp - grated cheese
- Butter to spread on slices
- 1 - cucumber thinly sliced
- I tbsp Salt
- Fresh ground black pepper

Preparation

1. Hold three slices at a time. Cut diagonally to get six triangles.
2. Keep each set of three separate, so they fit one on the other exactly.
3. Take the milk in a saucer. Make the sandwich using a cutting board.
4. Apply butter to the bread. Dip in the milk for 3 seconds and place it on the board. Spread some cheese. Sprinkle pepper and a pinch of salt.
5. Apply butter to the next slice—dip and place on first. Place cucumber slices on it. Sprinkle salt and pepper as before.
6. Apply butter to the third slice—dip and place on second.
7. Apply a dot of butter on top. Lift with a spatula and then place on a warmed griddle.
8. Toast the surfaces and sides until brown, turning to toast all over. Repeat for remaining sandwiches.
9. If the griddle is large, many can be done at a time. Serve hot with French fries, ketchup and decorated with thin cabbage strips.

Nutrition Facts

Calories: 240 Cal

Fat: 9 grams

Sodium: 154mg

Potassium: 37mg

Fiber: 1g

Sugar: 3g

Calcium: 13mg

Iron: 1mg

22. AMISH POTATO BREAD

Prep: 30 min

Rising Bake: 40 min

Ingredients

- 1/4-ounce active dry yeast
- 1/4 cup warm water (110° to 115°)
- 1-3/4 cups warm fat-free milk (110° to 115°)
- 1/3 cup butter, softened
- 1/4 cup mashed potatoes (without added milk and butter)
- 3 tablespoons sugar
- 1-1/2 teaspoons salt
- 1-1/2 cups whole wheat flour
- 3-1/2 to 4 cups all-purpose flour

Preparation

1. In a large bowl, dissolve yeast in warm water. Add the milk, butter, mashed potatoes, sugar, salt, whole wheat flour, and 1/2 cup all-purpose flour. Beat until smooth and stir in enough remaining flour to form a firm dough.
2. Turn onto a lightly floured surface. Knead until smooth and elastic, 6–8 minutes—place in a bowl coated with cooking spray, turning once to coat the top. Cover and let rise in a warm place until doubled, about 1 hour.
3. Punch down dough and turn onto a floured surface; shape into a loaf. Place in a 9x5-inch loaf pan coated with cooking spray. Cover and let rise for about 30 minutes until it doubles.
4. Bake for 45 minutes at 350° or until golden brown. Remove from pan, place on a wire rack to cool.

Nutrition Facts

Calories: 193

Fat: 4g

Cholesterol: 11mg

Sodium: 276mg

Carbohydrate: 33g

Protein: 6g

23. HOTTEOK

Prep: 40 mins

Cook: 10 mins

Total: 50 mins

Ingredients

- 2 ½ cups all-purpose flour
- 1 tablespoon instant dry yeast
- 2 teaspoons white sugar
- 1 cup milk
- ¼ cup water
- ¾ teaspoon salt
- ¾ cup packed brown sugar
- ¼ cup white sugar
- ¼ cup finely chopped walnuts
- ¼ cup black sesame seeds, ground
- 2 teaspoons ground cinnamon
- 2 tablespoons margarine

Preparation

1. Combine flour, yeast, and two teaspoons of white sugar in a bowl.
2. Stir water and milk together in a microwave-safe bowl, heat until lukewarm for 20 seconds. Pour milk mixture into the flour mixture. Mix with a fork; the dough will evenly combine.
3. Turn dough onto a lightly floured surface. Knead for 2 minutes- the dough will be sticky. Add salt to the dough and then knead until the dough is smooth for 2 minutes. Shape dough into a ball. Place it on a floured surface and cover with a wet paper towel. Let rise for 10 minutes.
4. Mix 1/4 cup white sugar, brown sugar, sesame seeds, cinnamon, and walnuts in a resealable plastic bag. Close bag and shake; filling will be evenly combined.
5. Roll the dough into a cylinder. Cut it into ten pieces, forming a ball. Using a rolling pin, roll into a 5-inch circle. Place it into the palm of your hand, spoon two tablespoons of filling into the middle of the dough. Wrap dough around the filling and form ball by taking four corners of the dough and pinching together in the middle. Take another four corners, pinch together, and seal them completely. Place the balls seam-side down onto a floured surface.
6. Proceed to roll each ball into a 5-inch circle using a rolling pin, ensuring filling stays in the dough.
7. Place margarine in a skillet. Spread the dough around with a paper towel; heat over medium heat. Place the dough in the melted margarine. Cook until golden brown for about 10 minutes per side.

Nutrition Facts

Carbohydrates: 48.3g

Dietary Fiber: 2g

Sugars: 22.4g

Protein: 5.6g

Fat: 6.7g

Cholesterol: 2mg

Calcium: 91.4mg

Potassium: 149mg

Sodium: 215.8mg

24. GOLDEN HONEY PAN ROLLS

Prep: 35 min.

Rising Bake: 20 min

Ingredients

- 1 large egg, room temperature
- 1 large egg yolk, room temperature
- 1 cup of warm 2% milk (70°C to 80°C)
- 3-1/2 cups bread flour
- 1/2 cup canola oil
- 2 tablespoons honey
- 1-1/2 teaspoons salt
- 2-1/4 teaspoons active dry yeast

Glaze

- 1/3 cup sugar
- 2 tablespoons butter, melted
- 1 tablespoon honey
- 1 large egg white
- Additional honey, optional

Preparation

1. Place the eight ingredients in order suggested by the manufacturer in the bread machine pan. Select the dough setting (check dough after about 5 minutes of mixing; add 1 or 2 tablespoons of water or flour if necessary).

2. When the cycle is complete, turn dough onto a lightly floured surface. Punch down the dough and cover it. Let it rest for about 10 minutes. Divide your dough into 24 pieces and shape them into balls. Place 12 balls each in two greased 8-inch square baking pans. Cover and let rise in a warm place until it doubles in about 30 minutes.

For the glaze

1. Combine butter, sugar, honey, and the egg white; drizzle it over the dough. Bake at 350°C until golden brown for 20-25 minutes. Brush with additional honey if desired

Nutrition Facts

Calories: 139

Fat: 6g

Cholesterol: 22mg

Sodium: 168mg

Carbohydrate: 18g

Protein: 3g.

25. BRAIDED SWEET MILK BREAD

Prep Time: 10 minutes

Cook Time: 14 minutes

Total Time: 24 minutes

Ingredients

- 2 ¼ cup flour
- ½ teaspoon salt
- 1 ½ teaspoon dry yeast
- 3 tablespoon sugar
- 1 whole egg at room temperature
- 1 tablespoon oil
- 1 tablespoon melted butter
- 6 tablespoon warm milk

Egg wash

- 1 egg yolk plus 2 tablespoons of milk

Preparation

1. Add yeast, milk, and sugar. Whisk well until the sugar dissolves in a bowl. Add the rest of the ingredients then, knead for two minutes; the dough will be very sticky at this point.
2. Grab your dough and bash it on your working surface; continue until the dough gets firmer; it might take three minutes.
3. In an oiled bowl, place the dough. Cover it to double in size for about 90 minutes. Punch it but do not knead it again. Cut your dough in half, then each half into another half.
4. Roll two halves into a long log about 15 - 16 inches. Make a cross-like shape from the two halves while holding the bottom log from two ends and overlap. Perform this to the top log, continue doing so. This will end up with the braid being created—Tuck the ends under the braid and with the remaining two halves. Cover and let it rise again for ¾ hours.
5. Preheat the oven to 180°C. Brush the braids with the egg wash and sprinkle sesame seed, nigella seeds, or poppy seed on top—Bake for 14 minutes.
6. Allow it to cool completely on a cooling rack.

Nutrition Facts

Calories: 1026 kcal

Carbohydrates: 196g

Protein: 24g

Fat: 14g

Cholesterol: 110mg

Fiber: 5g

Sugar: 53g

Calcium: 112mg

Iron: 9.1mg

26. BROWN SUGAR RAISIN BREAD

Prep time: 165 mins

Cook time: 20 mins

Total time: 3 hours 5 minutes

Ingredients

Yudane

- 50g bread flour
- 40g boiling water
- Bread dough
- 150g whole milk, chilled
- 15g Japanese brown sugar
- 3g instant dry yeast
- 10g unsalted butter, chilled
- 200g bread flour
- 1/4 tsp. salt
- 65g raisins

Topping

- Milk, for brushing
- Oats

Preparation

Make Yudane a day or night before.

1. Place the bread flour and add the hot boiling water into the bowl. Mix well, then cling wrap dough and place it in the fridge overnight.

Bread Dough

1. Pour milk into the inner bread pan of the bread machine. Add the yeast, sugar, and butter. Tear the Yudane into pieces and add it in, followed by bread, flour and salt. Turn on the bread machine to dough kneading mode or mix your dough in your mixer.
2. After kneading the dough for about 5 minutes, add in raisins.
3. The dough is mixed to the windowpane stage (or when bread machine kneading mode ends). Roll the dough into a round ball. Let proof for about 60 minutes. Place a piece of cling wrap cloth over the dough to prevent it from drying.
4. Punch dough down. Divide it into 12 portions with a scraper. Roll them into round balls of dough. Place them into a lined or greased 8"x8" baking tray. Place cling wrap or cloth over the tray—proof a second time for about 1 hour.

5. Just before proofing ends, preheat the oven to 180°C. Brush the top of each dough with milk and sprinkle with oats. Bake for about 20-25 mins.

Nutrition Facts

Calories: 427kcal

Carbohydrates: 75g

Protein: 13g

Fat: 7g

Cholesterol: 28mg

Sodium: 406mg

Potassium: 149mg

Fiber: 3g

Calcium: 42mg

Iron: 1mg

27. BLUE-RIBBON HERB ROLLS

Prep time: 40 min

Rising bake time: 15 min

Ingredients

- 4 ½ cups all-purpose flour
- ¼ cup honey
- 2 -(1/4 ounce each) active dry yeast
- 1/3 cup vegetable oil
- 1 teaspoon onion powder
- 4 cups whole wheat flour
- 2 teaspoons dill weed
- 2 ¾ cups warm water (110°C to 115°C), divided
- 2 teaspoons dried thyme
- 2 teaspoons dried basil
- 1 large egg, room temperature, beaten
- 1 tablespoon salt

Preparation

1. Dissolve the yeast in ½-cup warm water in a large bowl. Add the honey, oil, salt, whole-wheat flour, seasonings, egg, and remaining water. Beat it until it is smooth. Stir the mixture in adequate all-purpose flour to form a smooth dough.
2. Turn onto a floured surface; knead for 8 minutes until smooth and elastic. Place in a greased bowl, turning once to grease top. Cover and let rise in a warm place until doubled, 60 minutes.
3. Punch dough down, turn lightly sprinkled with flour. Divide it into six portions. Divide each into 24 pieces. Shape each into a 1-in. ball; place three balls in each greased muffin cup. Cover and let it rise for approximately 20-25 minutes.
4. Bake at 375°C for about 12-15 minutes or until the tops are golden brown. Remove from pans to wire racks.

Nutrition Facts

Calories: 94

Fat: 2g

Cholesterol: 4mg

Sodium: 150mg

Carbohydrate: 17g

Protein: 3g

28. PUMPKIN BREAD ROLLS

Prep time: 45 minutes

Cook time: 25 minutes

Additional time: 2 hours

Total time: 3 hours 10 minutes

Ingredients

- 7g fast-action dried yeast
- 1 tablespoon soft light brown sugar
- 500g strong white bread flour
- 150g pumpkin puree
- 1 ½ teaspoons pumpkin pie spice
- ¼ teaspoon ground turmeric
- 2 tablespoons olive oil
- 250ml whole milk plus
- 7 pecan nuts for the stalks
- 1 ¼ teaspoons fine salt

- 1 beaten egg to glaze the rolls
- 25g melted butter (optional)

Preparation

1. Lightly oil two large baking trays and line with baking parchment. Place the yeast, flour, brown sugar, pumpkin pie spice, salt, and turmeric in a bowl of a stand mixer fitted with a dough hook. Place the yeast and salt at opposite ends of the bowl to avoid killing the yeast. Stir to mix all the ingredients.
2. Gently heat the milk in a saucepan (small) and until it is warm. Remove the pan from the heat. Stir the olive oil and pumpkin puree until the mixture is smooth, then pour the wet ingredients over the flour mixture and knead at low speed for about 5 minutes. If making the dough by hand, stir the milk into the flour mixture with a wooden spoon, then turn the dough out onto a lightly floured work surface. Knead the dough for about 10 minutes.
3. Place the kneaded dough in a lightly oiled bowl, cover, and leave it for 1-2 hours until the dough has doubled inside.
4. Turn out onto a lightly oiled work surface when your dough has risen. Lightly knead for a minute or two. Divide your dough into 12 equal-sized pieces and shape each into a tight, smooth ball.
5. Lay a long piece of string (about 60cm in length) out on your work surface. Place the ball in the middle of the string, and then bring each end up and cross them over. Do not tighten the string around the dough too much. Repeat the crossing string over the dough until you mark out six sections. Place each ball on the baking trays. Repeat the procedure with the remaining balls. Loosely cover the pieces of dough with oiled cling film. Leave them to rise for about 45 minutes
6. Preheat the oven to 180°C. Beat the egg with the remaining tablespoon of milk and brush the rolls with the egg wash when the dough balls have risen. Place them in the oven and bake for about 20 minutes. Leave the rolls to cool for a few minutes. Carefully snip off the string and break the pecan nuts into thin pieces. Press each piece into the top of each pumpkin roll. If desired, brush them with the melted butter and serve warm with honey or maple butter.

Nutrition Facts

Calories: 227

Total Fat: 5g

Cholesterol: 18mg

Sodium: 251mg

Carbohydrates: 38g

Fiber: 2g

Sugar: 6g

Protein: 7g

29. PURPLE SWEET POTATO

Prep time: 5 mins

Cook time: 30 mins

Ingredients

Tangzhong

- 2 ½ tablespoons bread flour
- ½ cup water

Bread

- 2 ½ teaspoons instant yeast
- 2 3/4 cups bread flour
- 1 teaspoon pink salt
- 1 tablespoon purple sweet potato powder
- ½ cup soy milk warmed to approximately 110°F
- ¼ cup plant-based butter softened

Preparation

For Tangzhong

1. Whisk flour and water together in a saucepan. Place over medium-low heat on the stove. Cook, constantly whisking, until the mixture thickens into a pudding-like consistency for about 5 minutes. This is easily overcooked, so make sure to stay nearby and stir often. Another way to check it is finished is when the mixture reaches 149°F. Let it cool; then you can use it

For the Bread

1. Combine dry ingredients in a bowl. Add the roux and warm milk to the stand mixer bowl fitted with the hook attachment. Add the dry ingredients. Turn on the mixer, increase the speed to medium from low, and mix for 7 minutes. The gluten develops, and the dough will feel elastic.
2. Add the butter a tablespoon at a time and wait until it is fully incorporated before adding more. Mix for another 5 minutes until the butter is completely incorporated and the dough is smooth and feels elastic.
3. Shape the dough into a ball and transfer it to a greased bowl. Cover and let rise for about 60-90 minutes or until doubled in size.
4. Gently deflate the dough, divide it into four equal parts, and shape it into four balls. Cover and let rise for 15 minutes.
5. Using a rolling pin, roll out each into an oval. Fold the two short edges towards the center. You should end up with a rectangle. Roll your dough into a log and place it down the tin seal, starting from one short edge. Repeat with the remaining dough. Cover and let rise for about 50 minutes or until the dough reaches the border.
6. Preheat the oven to 350°F. Lightly grease a 10x4-bread loaf pan. Brush the bread with some soymilk. Bake for about 15 minutes, lower the heat to 325°F. Bake for another 12 minutes and then remove from oven. Let cool in the pan for about 10 minutes before transferring to a rack to cool down completely. Enjoy!

Nutrition Facts

Calories: 167 kcal

Carbohydrates: 26g

Protein: 4g

Fat: 5g

Potassium: 62mg

Cholesterol: 15mg

Sodium: 13mg

Fiber: 1g

30. PORTUGUESE SWEET BREAD ROLLS

Prep: 30 mins

Cook: 30 mins

Total: 1 hour

Ingredients

- 4 tablespoon butter
- 1/3 cup warm milk
- 3 eggs slightly beaten
- 2/3 cup sweetened condensed milk
- 3 ½ cups all-purpose flour
- 1 tablespoon lemon zest
- 2 tablespoon brown sugar packed
- 1/2 teaspoon salt
- 2 1/2 teaspoon active dry yeast
- 1 egg for egg wash
- sesame seeds optional

Preparation

1. Warm up the 75 ml of milk to warm to the touch in a bowl. Add the yeast and brown sugar to it. Stir it well with a fork and let the yeast activate.
2. Add the flour to the mixer. Add the lemon zest and salt to it.
3. Add the eggs, melted butter, yeast mixture, condensed milk, and stir everything together in another bowl.

4. Pour the wet ingredients over the dry ingredients. Mix them using the dough hook for about 3 minutes on medium speed; the dough will be sticky and elastic. Let it rise in a warm place.
5. Turn your dough to a clean surface; use flour if you need to. The more elastic and stickier, the easier it is to work with. Knead each dough and form it into a long roll that you must cut into 12 pieces.
6. Let it rest for some minutes, so they rise a bit more and then brush them with the egg wash. Sprinkle with sugar or sesame seeds.
7. Preheat the baking oven to 350 F degrees and bake for about 25 to 30 minutes.

Nutrition Facts

Calories: 257kcal

Carbohydrates: 40g

Protein: 8g

Fat: 7g

Cholesterol: 71mg

Sodium: 144mg

Potassium: 139mg

Calcium: 72mg

Iron: 2mg

Prep: 20 min

Rising Bake: 10 min

Ingredients

- 1 cup + 2 tablespoons water (70° to 80°C), divided
- 3 cups all-purpose flour
- 3 tablespoons brown sugar
- 1-1/2 teaspoons active dry yeast
- 2 quarts water
- 1/2 cup baking soda
- Coarse salt

Preparation

1. Place 1 cup of water and the next three ingredients suggested by the manufacturer in a bread machine pan —select dough setting. Check dough after 5 minutes of mixing; add 1 to 2 tablespoons of water or flour if needed.
2. When the cycle is completed, turn dough onto a lightly floured surface. Divide dough into eight balls. Roll each into a 20-inch rope and form into a pretzel shape.
3. Bring 2 quarts of water and the baking soda to a boil in a large saucepan. Drop the pretzels into boiling water, two at a time; boil for 15 seconds. Remove with a slotted spoon. Drain on paper towels. Place the pretzels on greased baking sheets.
4. Preheat oven to 425° and bake for 10 minutes; bake until golden brown. Spritz or lightly brush with the remaining two tablespoons of water. Sprinkle with salt.

Nutrition Facts

Calories: 193

Fat: 1g

Sodium: 380mg

Carbohydrate: 41g

Protein: 5g

32. PERSIAN FLATBREAD

Cook time: 30 mins

Total time: 4 hours

Yield: 2

Ingredients

- 1/4 teaspoons active dry yeast
- 1 tablespoon all-purpose flour
- 4 cups bread flour,
- 1 teaspoon vegetable oil, more may be required for greasing
- Semolina or cornmeal, for sprinkling
- Pinch of salt
- 1 teaspoon sugar
- 1 tablespoon nigella seeds
- 1 tablespoon sesame seeds

Preparation

1. Combine two cups of lukewarm water with the yeast in the bowl of a standing mixer fitted with the dough hook and let stand for 5 minutes.
2. Add the four cups of bread flour and two teaspoons of salt. Mix them at medium speed until a loose dough forms. Increase the speed from medium to high and mix until the dough is supple and smooth for 6 minutes. Transfer the dough to a lightly floured work surface. Knead for 1 minute and then transfer the dough to an oiled bowl, cover with plastic wrap. Let it stand in a draft-free spot until it doubled in volume for 60 minutes.
3. Punch down the dough to remove air and form it into two ovals. Transfer the ovals to an oiled baking sheet. Cover it with a sheet of oiled plastic wrap and let rise for 1 hour.
4. Meanwhile, combine the all-purpose flour with the sugar, one teaspoon of vegetable oil, and 1/2 cup of water in a small saucepan. Cook the flour paste over moderate heat. Keep whisking for about 2 minutes until it thickens. Let the flour paste cool.

5. Preheat the oven to 450°C and set a pizza stone on the lowest rack. Let the stone heat for approximately 30 minutes. Generously sprinkle a pizza peel with semolina. Punch down one piece of the dough and transfer it to a lightly floured work surface. Press your dough to a 14-by-5-inch rectangle, and then transfer to the peel. Ensure you shake the peel lightly to make sure the dough does non-stick, adding more semolina if necessary. Using your fingers, press five deep lengthwise ridges into the dough and rub about one-third of the flour paste over the surface. Sprinkle it with half of the sesame and nigella seeds. Slide the dough onto the hot stone. Bake your dough for about 20 minutes, until golden and risen. Repeat to make the second loaf.
6. Serve warm.

Nutrition Facts

Calories: 234

Total fat: 1g

Cholesterol: 0mg

Sodium: 456mg

Potassium: 102mg

Total carbohydrates: 47g

Dietary fiber: 1.9g

Sugars: 1.1g

Protein: 7.7g

33. SCOTTISH SHORTBREAD

Prep time: 15 min

Bake time: 20 min

Ingredients

- 2 cups butter, softened
- 1 cup packed brown sugar
- 4 to 4-1/2 cups all-purpose flour

Preparation

1. Preheat oven to 325°C. Cream butter and brown sugar until 5-7 minutes until light and fluffy. Add 3 ¾ cups flour; mix well. Turn dough onto a floured surface; knead for 5 minutes, adding enough remaining flour to form a soft dough.
2. On a sheet of parchment paper, roll dough to a 16x9-inch rectangle. Transfer to a baking sheet, cut into 3x1-inch strips and prick each cookie multiple times with a fork. Refrigerate for around 30 minutes or overnight.
3. Separate cookies and place 1 inch apart on ungreased baking sheets. Bake until cookies are lightly browned, 20–25 minutes. Transfer to wire racks to cool completely.

Nutrition Facts

Calories: 123

Fat: 8g

Cholesterol: 20mg

Sodium: 62mg

Carbohydrate: 12g

Protein: 1g

34. LEMON CRUMB MUFFINS

Prep: 25 min

Bake: 20 min

Ingredients

- 6 cups all-purpose flour
- 4 cups sugar
- 3/4 teaspoon baking soda
- 3/4 teaspoon salt
- 8 large eggs, room temperature
- 2 cups sour cream
- 2 cups butter, melted
- 3 tablespoons grated lemon zest
- 2 tablespoons lemon juice

Topping

- 3/4 cup all-purpose flour
- 3/4 cup sugar
- 1/4 cup cold butter, cubed

Glaze

- 1/2 cup sugar
- 1/3 cup lemon juice

Preparation

1. Combine the flour, sugar, baking soda, and salt in a large bowl. Combine the eggs, sour cream, lemon zest, butter, and juice in another bowl and then stir into dry ingredients until moistened. Fill the greased muffin cups three-fourths full.
2. Combine flour and sugar in a bowl; cut in butter until mixture resembles coarse crumbs. Sprinkle over batter.
3. Bake for about 25 minutes at 350°C or until a toothpick inserted in the center comes out clean. Cool for 5 minutes before removing from pans to wire racks. In a small bowl, whisk glaze ingredients; drizzle over warm muffins. Serve warm.

Nutrition Facts

Calories: 308

Fat: 13g

Cholesterol: 77mg

Sodium: 159mg

Carbohydrate: 43g

Protein: 4g

35. BUTTERY CORNBREAD

Prep: 15 min

Bake 25 min

Ingredients

- 2/3 cup butter, softened
- 1 cup sugar
- 3 large eggs, room temperature
- 1-2/3 cups 2% milk
- 2-1/3 cups all-purpose flour
- 1 cup cornmeal
- 4-1/2 teaspoons baking powder
- 1 teaspoon salt

Preparation

1. Mix cream butter and sugar until light and fluffy for 7 minutes in a large bowl. Add a combination of eggs and milk.
2. Combine cornmeal, flour, baking powder, and salt and then add to creamed mixture alternately with egg mixture.
3. Preheat oven to 400°C. Pour into a greased 13x9-inch baking pan. Bake your dough for about 30 minutes or until a toothpick inserted in the center comes out clean.
4. Cut into squares; serve warm.

Nutrition Facts

Calories: 259

Fat: 10g

Cholesterol: 68mg

Sodium: 386mg

Carbohydrate: 37g

Protein: 5g

36. FRESH PEAR BREAD

Prep time: 15 min

Bake time: 55 min

Ingredients

- 3 large eggs, room temperature
- 1-1/2 cups sugar
- 3/4 cup vegetable oil
- 1 teaspoon vanilla extract
- 3 cups all-purpose flour
- 2 teaspoons baking powder
- 2 teaspoons ground cinnamon
- 1 teaspoon baking soda
- 1 teaspoon salt
- 4 cups finely chopped peeled ripe pears
- 1 teaspoon lemon juice

- 1 cup chopped walnuts

Preparation

1. Combine the eggs, sugar, oil, and vanilla; mix well. Combine flour, baking powder, cinnamon, baking soda, and salt; stir into the egg mixture just until moistened—Toss pears with lemon juice. Stir pears and walnuts into the batter (batter will be thick).
2. Spoon into two greased 9x5-inch loaf pans. Bake at 350°C for 60 minutes or until a toothpick inserted in the center comes out clean.
3. Cool the dough for approximately 10 minutes before removing pans to wire racks.

Nutrition Facts

Calories: 168

Fat: 8g

Cholesterol: 20mg

Sodium: 144mg

Carbohydrate: 22g

Protein: 3g

37. JAPANESE MILK BREAD

Preparation time: 20 mins

Cook time: 30 mins

Rise time: 1 hour 40 mins

Total time: 50 mins

Ingredients

Tangzhong

- 6 tablespoon water
- 2 tablespoon bread flour

Bread

- ½ cup of milk (lukewarm or room temperature)
- 300g bread flour
- 3 tablespoon sugar (caster sugar/fine)
- 2 teaspoons fast-acting yeast
- 1 teaspoon of salt
- 2tablespoon unsalted butter (melted but not hot)

- 1 egg

Glaze

- 1 egg (lightly beaten)

Preparation

For tangzhong – made ahead of time

1. In a small pan, put water and flour for tangzhong. Before turning on the heat, mix until smooth and no lumps remain.
2. Warm the flour paste gently over medium-low heat until it thickens, stirring constantly. Whisk as you stir and set the pan aside to cool.

Bread making

1. Measure out the remaining ingredients (flour, milk, sugar, melted butter, yeast, salt, and egg) into a large bowl. Beat an egg. Add it to the cooled tangzhong. Mix well. Mix all your ingredients by hand or using a mixer on a floured surface. Add a little more flour if needed.
2. Ensure the dough is no longer sticky. Transfer the dough into a lightly oiled bowl and then cover. Leave to rise in a warm place; it will double for an hour.
3. After rising, knock back the dough. Divide it into three pieces; set the two pieces to one side and roll the other into an oval.
8. Fold one side of dough over halfway across the remaining dough. Fold the other side on top to have three layers. Gently roll slightly, and then roll up the piece of dough as you would a cinnamon roll.
9. Repeat with the other pieces of dough. Put all three dough rolls in an oiled loaf pan - 9x5in or slightly smaller.
10. Cover and leave to rise again; the loaf will reach the top of the pan. Pre-heat the oven to 175C. Lightly beat the egg and then brush the top of the loaf with egg wash.
11. Bake the loaf for 30 minutes; it will be golden brown; if it changes to brown too fast, tent with foil. This is done in the last part of cooking. Place it onto a cooling rack to cool before slicing.

Nutrition Facts

Calories: 103kcal

Carbohydrates: 17g

Protein: 3g

Fat: 2g

Cholesterol: 15mg

Sugar: 3g

Calcium: 24mg

Iron: 2mg

38. JAPANESE MILK BREAD ROLLS

Preparation time: 30 mins

Bake time: 25 to 30 mins

Total time: 3 hours 57 mins

Tangzhong

- 3 tablespoons of whole milk
- 3 tablespoons of water
- 2 tablespoons of unbleached bread flour

Dough

- 2 ½ cups of unbleached bread flour
- 2 tablespoons of non-fat dry milk or baker's special dry milk
- ¼ cup (50g) sugar
- ½ cup of whole milk
- 4 tablespoons of unsalted butter, melted
- 1 tablespoon instant yeast
- 1 teaspoon of salt
- 1 large egg

Preparation

Making the tangzhong

1. Weigh your flour, and then sweep off any excess. Combine all ingredients in a small saucepan. Whisk until no lumps remain.
2. Place the saucepan over low heat. Cook the mixture, while constantly whisking, until thick and the whisk leaves lines on the bottom of the pan, about 5 minutes, and then transfer the tangzhong to a mixing bowl.
3. Let it cool to room temperature.

Making the dough

1. Mix the tangzhong with the other remaining ingredients and knead using a mixer, bread machine, or hand until a smooth, elastic dough forms.
2. Shape the dough into a ball. Let the dough rest in a lightly oiled bowl for about 75 minutes, making it puffy but not necessarily doubled in bulk.
3. Gently deflate the dough. Divide it into ten equal pieces (for medium-sized rolls or eight equal pieces (for large rolls). Shape each piece into a ball.

4. Place them into a lightly greased round 8" or 9-inch cake pan. Cover the pan. Let the rolls rest for 50 minutes-until puffy.
5. Preheat your oven to 350°F. Brush the bread rolls with egg wash or milk. Bake for 25 minutes; the rolls will turn golden brown on top.
6. Remove the bread rolls from the oven. Allow the bread rolls to cool in the pan for 10 minutes. Transfer them to a rack to allow them to cool completely.

Nutrition Facts

Calories: 250 Cal

Total Fat: 8g

Cholesterol: 40mg

Sodium: 320mg

Total carbohydrate: 37g

Protein: 8g

39. WOOL ROLL MILK BREAD WITH CHAR SIU FILLING (TANGZHONG)

Prep time: 30 minutes

Cook time: 30 minutes

Total time: 1 hour

Servings: 8

Ingredients

Water roux

- 15g bread flour
- 90 ml whole milk

Char Siu filling

- 1 small onion
- 1 tablespoon oil
- 1 tablespoon soy sauce
- 1 tablespoon oyster sauce
- 2 tablespoon all-purpose flour
- 2 tablespoon hoisin sauce

- 500g Chinese BBQ pork dice into small pieces.
- 1 tsp. sesame oil
- 2 tablespoon sugar or more to taste 1 tablespoon red yeast rice powder optional

Dry ingredients

- 5g instant yeast
- 300g bread flour
- 5g milk powder

Wet ingredients

- 120 ml whole milk
- 1 large egg lightly beaten

Ingredient to add last to the dough

- 40g butter softened
- ¾ tsp. salt
- 2 tablespoon sugar

Egg wash

- 1 egg beaten

Preparation

Char Siu filling

1. Preheat a pan. Add cooking oil, then onion, and stir while frying until they are soft, for 3 minutes. Add the BBQ pork and the rest of the ingredients (except for all-purpose flour) while stirring until the sugar melts and the seasonings coat the pork pieces. Add more sugar and/or salt to adjust the taste. When satisfied with the taste, sprinkle in the flour and keep stirring; the mixture will be pastier and stickier. Remove from the heat. Let it cool down before using. The filling can be prepared a few days before and refrigerated for up to one week
2. When ready to use, divide the filling into five equal portions.

Tangzhong

1. Place the bread flour and milk in a saucepan and whisk until there are no more lumps. Cook the mixture for 5 minutes over medium heat until thickened. Remove from the heat. Let it cool down completely

Prepare the dough

1. Combine all the dry ingredients, then make a well at the center and pour the wet ingredients and the tangzhong you prepared earlier into a mixing bowl. Use a dough hook attachment to knead your dough until all the crumbly dough starts to come together into one mass; this will take about 3 minutes. Stop it halfway and scrape your dough off the hook and the sides of the bowl and knead several times again
2. Once it forms a dough, stop the machine. Cover the dough. Let it rest for 20 minutes.

3. After resting, turn on and knead the dough again. Knead for 2 minutes and add the sugar and salt into the dough. Continue kneading until the dough is relatively smooth. Stop and scrape the dough off the hook and the bowl several times.
4. Once you have a smooth dough, start the machine again to knead and gradually add in the softened butter a bit; the dough will be very sticky because of the butter. Keep kneading, stop halfway, and scrape the dough off the hook and bowl again. Continue kneading until the dough absorbs the butter.

First proofing

1. Place the dough in a lightly oiled large bowl; cover it with a clean and damp tea cloth. Let it rise in a warm place for about 1 hour or longer

Fill and shape

1. Line an 8-inch round pan with parchment paper on the bottom, divide your dough into five equal pieces. Work with a single dough at a time while keeping the rest covered. Roll the dough out into a rectangle of about 10 x 5 inches. Use a knife to cut it into thin strips along the upper half of the dough. Ensure you cut through for the wool.
2. Spread the char siu filling on the bottom half and leave about a 1/2-inch gap on the edge. Fold the edge over a bit, and then start rolling each from the bottom to the top. Place it inside the perimeter of the round pan—Preheat for the rest of the dough and filling.

Second proofing

1. Cover the dough using a damp cloth, place it in a warm place and let them rise for 60 minutes.

Baking

1. Ten minutes before the end of the second proofing, preheat the oven at 170° C and brush the bread with egg wash. Put the pan in the oven's middle rack to bake for 30 minutes; the bread will be golden brown. Let the bread dough rest inside the pan for 3 minutes, and then loosen the edge. Remove the dough from the pan onto a cooling rack and let them cool down completely

Nutrition Facts

Calories: 355kcal

Carbohydrates: 53g

Protein: 19g

Fat: 7g

Cholesterol: 36mg

Sodium: 742mg

Potassium: 121mg

Sugar: 21g

40. LIGHT WHEAT SOURDOUGH WOOL ROLL BREAD (TANGZHONG)

Prep time: 4–8 hours

Bake time: 3–4 hours

Servings: 1 loaf

Ingredients

Sweet Levain

- ½ cup all-purpose or whole wheat flour
- 1/4 cup of milk, warm
- 2 tablespoon fed and active sourdough starter
- 1 tsp. of sugar

Tangzhong

- 3 tablespoon all-purpose or whole wheat flour
- 1/2 cup of milk, or 60g water/60g milk

Dough

- 2 ¼ cups all-purpose flour
- ¼ cup of granulated sugar
- ¾ tsp. of salt
- ¼ cup milk, warm
- 1 egg, lightly beaten
- ¼ cup of butter, room temperature

Wash

- 1 tablespoon milk

Preparation

Make the sweet levain

1. Combine the sourdough starter, warm milk, flour, and sugar until combined in a small bowl. Cover the bowl and let the combination rise for about 4 – 8 hours at warm room temperature until it doubles in size. Make the tangzhong.
2. Whisk together milk and the flour until smooth in a small saucepan. Bring the combination to a simmer over medium-low heat and continue whisking until the mixture thickens. To determine when it is ready, whisk along the bottom of the pan. This will take about 5-10 minutes, leaving an indentation.
3. Pour the mixture and cover with plastic wrap and allow cooling at room temperature. into a small bowl.

Dough

1. Add the flour, beaten egg, sugar, salt, tangzhong, and levain in a large mixing bowl and whisk. Mix until it forms a shaggy dough.
2. Using your fingers, mix in the softened butter a little at a time. Cover the bowl. Let it sit for 45 minutes. Stretch your dough and fold it to help develop the gluten by lifting it and folding it over several times while turning the bowl; the dough will still feel shaggy. Cover it and let your dough rest for about 2-3 hours. Stretch and folds every 45 minutes for a total of about 3-4 stretches and folds; the dough will become more developed with each stretch and fold. Using plastic wrap, cover the bowl tightly and place it in the refrigerator for 8 hours and up to 24 hours.
3. If desired, grease the bottom and sides of a cake pan or a springform pan and line with parchment paper.
4. Divide your dough into six pieces, then roll each into a thin, oblong shape, using a sharp knife, pizza cutter, or bench scraper, starting about ⅔s from the designated top and making ⅛" to ¼" cuts.
5. Add a filling if using one, begin rolling from the solid top, ending at the bottom. Carefully place it in the pan, cover it, and let the dough rise until doubled in size.
6. Before the rising time's end, preheat the oven to 350 F. When using filling, place your pan on a rimmed baking sheet top to catch the goodness that oozes out. Brush the bread with milk. Bake your dough on the middle rack for approximately 35 minutes, rotating the pan partway through for even baking.
7. Let the bread cool in the pan for 10-15 minutes. Remove the loaf to a wire rack to continue cooling. Enjoy!

Nutrition Facts

Calories: 386

Total Fat: 7g

Protein: 9g

Cholesterol: 15mg

Sodium: 194mg

Carbohydrates: 72g

Fiber: 3g

Sugar: 6g

41. NORWEGIAN SCHOOL BREAD

Prep: 2 hours

Cook: 15 mins

Total: 2 hours 15 mins

Ingredients

- 4 cups all-purpose flour
- 2 ¼ teaspoons active dry yeast,
- shredded coconut
- ½ cup sugar
- 1 ½ cups milk
- 1 large egg, well beaten
- 6 tablespoons confectioners' sugar
- 1/4 cup unsalted butter
- 2 teaspoons freshly ground cardamom
- 5.1-ounce instant vanilla pudding mix
- 1 tablespoon water

Preparation

1. Combine butter and milk, heat in a saucepan over medium-high heat until milk is scalded. Remove it from heat. Let it cool until "finger-warm." Stir sugar and yeast into lukewarm milk. Allow sitting for about 10 minutes; the surface should begin to bubble as yeast proofs.
2. After 10 minutes, stir in flour and cardamom until dough pulls away from the sides of the mixing bowl. Using a clean kitchen towel, cover the bowl with and rise until doubled, about 1 hour.
3. Punch down your dough when it has risen, remove it to a floured surface, and knead until smooth and shiny.
4. Roll dough into a thick 18-inch-long "snake" using your hands and then cut this length into 20 equal pieces.
5. Roll each piece of your dough between hands into a spherical bun and place it on a lightly greased baking sheet. Cover buns again with the towel and rise until it doubles for about 30 minutes.
6. Prepare the pudding mix as directed, only reducing milk to 2 ½ cups. Allow pudding to thicken at room temperature while buns rise.
7. Preheat oven to 375 F. Gently press down the center of each bun to form a well after they have risen. Fill with 1 to 1 ½ tablespoon of pudding. Allow rising for an additional 10 minutes.
8. Brush the burns with a well-beaten egg onto the edges and its sides. Bake for 15 minutes, until golden brown. Remove from oven and allow cooling.
9. Mix the water with confectioners' sugar and then brush the sugar glaze on top of buns, around but not over pudding "eye." in a small bowl dipped into shredded coconut.

Nutrition Facts

Total fat: 4g

Saturated fat: 3g

Cholesterol: 17mg

Sodium: 130mg

Total carbohydrate: 40g

Protein: 4g

Calcium: 30mg

Iron: 1mg

Potassium: 79mg

42. SWEET POTATO CINNAMON BREAD

Prep: 20 min

Bake: 35 min

Ingredients

3-1/2 cups all-purpose flour

2-2/3 cups sugar

2 teaspoons baking soda

1 teaspoon salt

1/2 teaspoon baking powder

1-1/2 teaspoons ground cinnamon

1 teaspoon ground ginger

1/2 teaspoon ground cloves

4 large eggs, room temperature

2 cups mashed sweet potatoes

2/3 cup canola oil

2/3 cup 2% milk

1-1/2 cups raisins

1 cup chopped walnuts

Preparation

1. Whisk the first eight ingredients in a large bowl. Whisk eggs, oil, sweet potatoes, and milk in another bowl until blended. Add to flour mixture and then stir just until moistened. Fold in raisins and walnuts.
2. Transfer to 4 greased 5-3/4x3x2-inch loaf pans.
3. Preheat oven to 350° and bake for about 35-40 minutes or until a toothpick inserted in the center comes out clean. Cool in pans for 10 minutes before removing to wire racks to cool.

Nutrition Facts

Calories: 299

Fat: 10g

Cholesterol: 36mg

Sodium: 236mg

Carbohydrate: 49g

Protein: 4g

43. CHOCOLATE BABKA

Prep: 20 min

Bake: 35 min

Ingredients

- 4 ¾ cups all-purpose flour
- ½ cup sugar
- ½ cup water
- ¾ teaspoon salt
- 3 large eggs
- 1 large egg yolk, beaten (room temperature)
- 2/3 cup butter
- 2 ½ teaspoons quick-rise yeast
- 2 tablespoons grated orange zest

Filling

- 5 ounces dark chocolate chips
- ½ cup confectioners' sugar
- ¼ teaspoon salt
- 1/3 cup baking cocoa
- ½ cup butter, cubed

Glaze

- ¼ cup water
- ¼ cup sugar

Preparation

1. Mix two cups of flour, yeast sugar, and salt in a large bowl. Cut in butter until crumbly. Heat water to 120°C-130°C in a small saucepan, stir into dry ingredients. Stir in orange zest, eggs, yolk, and enough remaining flour to form a sticky dough.
2. Turn your dough onto a floured surface, and then knead until it is smooth and elastic for 8 minutes. Place the dough in a greased bowl, turning once to grease the top. Cover and refrigerate for about 8 hours or overnight.
3. Divide in half. Roll each half into a 12x10-in. rectangle. For the filling, melt butter and chocolate chips; stir until smooth—stir in cocoa, confectioners' sugar, and salt. Spread filling to within ½ inch of edges. Roll up jelly-roll style, starting with a long side; pinch seam and ends to seal.
4. Cut each roll lengthwise in half; carefully turn each half-cut side up. Loosely twist strips around each other, keeping cut surfaces facing up; pinch ends together to seal. Place in two greased 9x5-in. loaf pans cut side up and cover them with kitchen towels; let rise in a warm place until almost doubled, about 1 hour—Preheat oven to 375°C.
5. Bake until golden brown for about 45 minutes, tenting with foil halfway through baking. Meanwhile, combine sugar and water; bring to a boil. Reduce heat; simmer, uncovered, for 10 minutes. Brush over warm babka and cool for 10 minutes before removing pans to wire racks.

Nutrition Facts

Calories: 181

Fat: 9g

Cholesterol: 41mg

Sodium: 136mg

Carbohydrate: 23g

Protein: 3g

44. SUNFLOWER SEED & HONEY WHEAT BREAD

Prep: 40 min

Rising bake: 35 min

Ingredients

- ¼ cup bread flour
- 2 -(1/4 ounce each) active dry yeast
- 3-1/4 cups warm water (110°C to 115°C)
- 1/3 cup honey
- 1/3 cup canola oil
- 3 teaspoons salt
- 7 ½ cups whole wheat flour
- 3 tablespoons butter, melted
- ½ cup sunflower kernels

Preparation

1. Dissolve yeast in warm water in a large bowl. Add the bread flour, honey, oil, salt, and four whole-wheat flour cups. Beat until smooth. Stir in sunflower kernels and enough remaining flour to form a firm dough.
2. Turn onto a floured surface; knead for 7 minutes until smooth and elastic. Place in a greased bowl, turning once to grease the top; cover and let rise in a warm place for an hour.
3. Punch dough down; divide into three portions. Shape into loaves; place in 3 greased 8x4-inch loaf pans; cover and let rise for 30 minutes.
4. Bake the dough at 350°C for 35-40 minutes until the bread is golden brown. Brush with melted butter and then remove from pans to wire racks to cool.

Nutrition Facts

Fat: 4g

Calories: 125

Cholesterol: 3mg

Sodium: 212mg

Carbohydrate: 19g

Protein: 4g

45. POPPY SEED BREAD WITH ORANGE GLAZE

Prep: 20 min

Bake 55 min

Ingredients

- 3 cups all-purpose flour
- 2-1/4 cups sugar
- 3 teaspoons baking powder
- 1-1/2 teaspoons salt
- 3 large eggs, room temperature
- 1-1/2 cups whole milk
- 1 cup canola oil
- 1 tablespoon plus 1-1/2 teaspoons poppy seeds
- 1-1/2 teaspoons each butter flavoring, almond extract, and vanilla extract

Glaze

- 3/4 cup confectioners' sugar
- 1/4 cup orange juice
- 1/2 teaspoon each butter flavoring, almond extract, and vanilla extract

Preparation

1. Combine the baking powder, flour, sugar, and salt in a bowl. Whisk the eggs, milk, oil, poppy seeds, butter flavoring, and extracts in a small bowl. Stir into dry ingredients just until moistened.
2. Transfer to two greased and floured 9x5-inch loaf pans. Bake for 55-60 minutes at 350° until a toothpick inserted in the center comes out clean.
3. Cool it for about 10 minutes before removing it from pans to wire racks. Combine glaze ingredients; drizzle over warm loaves.

Nutrition Facts

Calories: 190

Fat: 8g

Cholesterol: 21mg

Sodium: 160mg

Carbohydrate: 27g

Protein: 2g

46. FIVE SPICE GARLIC BUTTER SCALLION MILK BREAD

Prep time: 17 minutes

Cook time: 40 minutes

Bread proof time: 2 hours

Total time: 2 hours 57 mins

Ingredients

Tangzhong

- 3 tablespoon flour
- 6 tablespoon milk

Five-spice scallion milk bread

- ½ cup milk warmed to 30°C
- 320g all-purpose flour
- 7g active dry yeast
- ¼ cup granulated sugar
- 4 tablespoon butter (room temperature)
- 1½ tablespoon five-spice powder
- 1 tsp. kosher salt
- 2 tablespoon minced garlic
- 4 tablespoon melted butter
- 2 eggs, room temperature (one for the egg wash and one for the dough)

- 5 stalks scallions, one stalk for topping the slices of bread

Equipment

- Bowl for proofing
- 2 loaf pans
- Mixer
- Pastry brush
- parchment paper + non-stick spray
- Rolling pin
- Bench scraper
-

Preparation

1. In a saucepan, combine flour and milk. Place it on medium heat. Whisk it constantly for two minutes until the mixture turns into a paste.
2. At the same time, heat your milk in a measuring cup over medium heat in a pot of water.
3. Set the tangzhong aside to allow cooling. Add the yeast to the warmed milk. Allow the yeast to bloom for about 10 minutes; this will double its size.
4. Prepare the dough by combining flour, salt, and sugar in your mixer bowl as the yeast blooms.
5. When ready, on the low-speed setting (2). Combine dry mix with tangzhong, the egg, and the milk and yeast mixture, then knead until everything has been incorporated; this might take about five minutes.
6. Increase speed to medium (4) and knead the dough for 5 minutes until smooth. Add in 4 tablespoons of butter in 1 tablespoon blocks.
7. Once done, remove the dough from the mixer bowl. Gently shape your dough into a ball while holding it, and then place the dough ball into a greased bowl. Cover with plastic or a tea towel and proof for about 2 hours. The dough has doubled.
8. Prepare your loaf pans while the dough rises by spraying non-stick and lining them with parchment. Before you roll out your dough, combine melted butter with the five-spice and minced garlic.
9. Once doubled, transfer the dough to a lightly floured work surface. Cut it into half and roll the two doughs out to around 7 inches x 13 inches. Position the dough with the 7-inch width facing you. Brush on the five-spice garlic butter and then top with the chopped scallions (4 stalks).
10. Carefully roll the dough into a bit of a log by rolling top-down or bottom-up.
11. Once rolled, place it seam side down. Using a knife, slice your dough log like you would a hassel-back potato. Slicing it almost down but leaving the bottom attached, then transferring the two loaves into their loaf pans. Cover and let rise for an hour.
12. Heat oven to 350°F and beat an egg and brush it over the risen loaves. Top with more sliced scallions.
13. Bake the loaves for 35 minutes on the low rack of your oven.
14. When done, let cool before slicing. Enjoy!

Nutrition Facts

Carbohydrates: 86g

Cholesterol: 105mg

Protein: 15.2g

Sugar: 14g

Calories: 637kcal

Fat: 25.6g

Saturated Fat: 10g

Fiber: 3.2g

Sodium: 435mg

47. ROSEMARY WALNUT BREAD

Prep: 25 min

Rising Bake: 20 min

Ingredients

- 1 ¼ teaspoons active dry yeast
- 1/2 cup warm water (110° to 115°)
- 1/4 cup whole wheat flour
- 1 ¾ cups all-purpose flour
- 2 tablespoons honey
- 1 tablespoon olive oil
- 1 ½ teaspoons dried rosemary, crushed
- 1/2 teaspoon salt
- 1/3 cup finely chopped walnuts

Preparation

1. dissolve yeast in warm water in a small bowl. Mix whole-wheat flour and 1/4 cup all-purpose flour; stir in yeast mixture in another bowl. Let stand, covered, for 15 minutes. Add honey, oil, rosemary, salt, and 3/4 cup all-purpose flour; beat on medium speed until smooth. Stir in walnuts and enough remaining all-purpose flour to form a soft dough.
2. Turn dough onto a floured surface; knead until smooth and elastic, 6-8 minutes. Place in a greased bowl, turning once to grease the top. Cover and let rise in a warm place until doubled, about 45 minutes.
3. Punch down dough. Turn onto a lightly floured surface; divide into thirds. Roll each into a 12-in. rope—place ropes on a greased baking sheet and braid. Pinch ends to seal; tuck under. Cover with a kitchen towel; let rise for about 30 minutes in a warm place until it almost doubles.
4. Preheat oven to 375°C and bake for 20-25 minutes or until it turns golden brown. Remove it from the pan; place it on a wire rack to cool.

Nutrition Facts

Calories: 145

Fat: 4g

Sodium: 132mg

Carbohydrate: 23g

Protein: 4g

48. FOCACCIA

Prep: 30 min

Rising bake: 15 min

Ingredients

- 3 cups all-purpose flour
- 1 ¼ cups warm water (110°C to 115°C), divided
- 1 tablespoon honey
- ¼ ounce active dry yeast
- ¾ teaspoon kosher salt
- ¼ cup plus 3 tablespoons olive oil, divided
- 1 teaspoon flaky sea salt, optional

Preparation

1. Dissolve the yeast in ½ cup of warm water and honey. Let it stand for about 5 minutes. Add flour, salt, 1/4 cup oil, and the remaining 3/4 cup water. Mix until smooth
2. Scrape the sides of the bowl clean. Cover and let rise for about 50 minutes in a warm place.
3. Preheat oven to 425°. Brush a 13x9-inch baking dish with one tablespoon of oil. Gently scrape dough directly into the pan. With oiled hands, gently spread the dough. If dough springs back, wait for about 10 minutes and stretch again. Using your fingers, make some indentations in the dough. Drizzle with the remaining two tablespoons oil; let rise until doubled in size, 30-40 minutes.
4. If desired, sprinkle with sea salt. Bake until golden brown, 20-25 minutes. Cut into squares; serve warm.

Nutrition Facts

Calories: 95

Fat: 4g

Sodium: 61mg

Carbohydrate: 13g

Protein: 2g

49. SOFT POPPY SEED MILK BREAD

Prep time: 30 minutes

Proof Time: 3 hours

Baking Time: 35 minutes

Ingredients

- 1/4 cup shortening
- 1/4 cup white sugar
- 1/4 tsp. yeast
- 1 tsp. salt
- 1 egg, beaten
- 3 cups bakers' flour
- 3 1/2 cups plain flour
- Poppy seeds

Preparation

1. Heat milk until it is hot; do not boil in a saucepan - take off the stove. Add the sugar and shortening, then stir. Set aside until shortening has melted and the mixture is tepid/warm.
2. Add yeast, beaten egg, and salt, then slowly add and mix in the bakers' flour until smooth. Set aside for 10 minutes.
3. Put plain flour in your stand mixer. Gradually add the wet ingredients to the bowl until all combined, and then knead for 5 minutes in your mixer on the lowest setting or 10 minutes by hand. The mixture should be elastic in texture.
4. Grease two bowls with kitchen spray. Divide the mixture into each, spray the top of the mixture lightly with kitchen spray, and then cover with cling film. Leave to prove until it doubles in size for about 1 - 3 hours.
5. Once it doubles in size, preheat the oven to 200°C.
6. Take out, roll into the shape of your bread tins and then roll in poppy seeds. Score diagonally onto the account for rising to prevent splitting. Bake in the oven for 30-35 minutes.
7. Take out of the tin, cool on a raised tray before slicing and serving.

Nutrition Facts

Calories: 372

Total Fat: 17g

Saturated Fat: 7.3g

Sodium: 214mg

Total Carbohydrates: 48g

Sugars: 13g

Protein: 8.3g

50. TOMATO-HERB FOCACCIA

Prep: 30 min

Rising Bake: 20 min

Ingredients

- 1/4-ounce active dry yeast
- 1 cup warm water (110° to 115°)
- 1 teaspoon sugar
- 2 tablespoons olive oil, divided
- 1 ½ teaspoons salt
- 1 teaspoon each dried thyme, oregano, and rosemary(crushed)
- Dash pepper
- 2 ½ cups all-purpose flour
- 1 teaspoon garlic powder
- 1/2 teaspoon dried basil
- 2 plum tomatoes, thinly sliced
- 1/4 cup shredded part-skim mozzarella cheese
- 1 tablespoon grated Parmesan cheese

Preparation

1. In a large bowl, dissolve yeast in warm water. Add 1 tablespoon oil, salt, sugar, garlic powder, herbs, pepper, and 1 ½ cups flour. Beat until smooth. Stir in enough remaining flour to form a soft dough (dough will be sticky).
2. Turn onto a floured surface; knead until smooth and elastic, about 6-8 minutes. Place in a greased bowl, turning once to grease the top. Cover and let rise in a warm place until doubled, about 1 hour.
3. Punch dough down. Cover and let rest for 10 minutes. Shape into a 13-inch x 9-inch rectangle; place on a greased baking sheet. Cover and let rise for about 30 minutes until it doubles. With fingertips, make several dimples over top of the dough.
4. Brush it with remaining oil; arrange tomatoes over the top. Sprinkle with cheeses. Bake for 20–25 minutes at 400°C or until golden brown. Remove to a wire rack.

Nutrition Facts

Calories: 112

Fat: 3g

Cholesterol: 2mg

Sodium: 320mg

Carbohydrate: 18g

Protein: 3g

51. WILD RICE & CRANBERRY LOAVES

Prep: 40 min

Rising Bake: 40 min

Ingredients

- 2 cups whole wheat flour
- 2 packages (1/4 ounce each) quick-rise yeast
- 1 tablespoon sugar
- 1 tablespoon grated orange zest
- 2 teaspoons aniseed
- 1 teaspoon salt
- 1 teaspoon caraway seeds
- 4 ½ cups bread flour
- 2 cups 2% milk
- ½ cup water
- 1/4 cup molasses
- 2 tablespoons butter

- 1 cup dried cranberries
- 1 cup cooked wild rice, cooled

Preparation

1. Mix the first seven ingredients and 1 ½ cups of bread flour in a large bowl: heat milk, water, molasses, and butter in a small saucepan to 120°–130°C.
2. Add the mixture to the dry ingredients, then beat on medium speed for 2 minutes. Stir in cranberries, rice, and enough remaining bread flour to form a stiff dough (dough will be sticky).
3. Turn dough onto a floured surface; knead until smooth and elastic, about 6–8 minutes. Place in a greased bowl, turning once to grease the top. Cover with plastic wrap and let rest for 10 min.
4. Punch it down; turn it onto a lightly floured surface. Divide in half and shape into loaves. Place in two greased 9x5-inch loaf pans, seam side down. Cover with kitchen towels; let rise for about 20 minutes in a warm place until almost doubled,
5. Preheat oven to 350°C. Bake for 40–45 minutes or until golden brown.
6. Cool in pans for 10 minutes; remove to wire racks to cool completely.

52. ORANGE CRANBERRY BREAD

Prep: 20 min

Bake: 50 min

Ingredients

- 2 ¾ cups all-purpose flour
- 2/3 cup sugar
- 2/3 cup packed brown sugar
- 3 ½ teaspoons baking powder
- 1 teaspoon salt
- 1/2 teaspoon ground cinnamon
- 1/4 teaspoon ground nutmeg
- 1 large egg, room temperature
- 3 tablespoons canola oil
- 1 large apple, peeled and chopped
- 1 cup 2% milk
- 1/2 cup orange juice
- 2 cups coarsely chopped frozen or fresh cranberries
- 3 teaspoons grated orange zest

Preparation

1. Combine the flour, baking powder, sugars, cinnamon, salt, and nutmeg in a large bowl. Whisk the egg, orange juice, milk, oil, and orange zest; stir into dry ingredients just until blended. Fold in the apple and cranberries.
2. Pour into two greased 8x4-inch loaf pans. Bake for 50-55 minutes at 350℃ or until a toothpick inserted in the center comes out clean. Cool for 10 minutes before removing from pans to wire racks.

Nutrition Facts

Calories: 98

Fat: 2g

Cholesterol: 8mg

Sodium: 125mg

Carbohydrate: 19g

Sugars: 10g

Protein: 2g.

53. SWEET MILK DINNER ROLLS

Prep: 20 min

Rising Bake: 35 min

Ingredients

- 5 cups all-purpose flour
- 2 cups of warm 2% milk (110°C to 115°C)
- 2 tablespoons butter, melted
- ¼ ounce active dry yeast
- 1 teaspoon salt
- ½ cup sugar

Preparation

1. Dissolve the yeast in warm milk in a large bowl. Add three cups flour, butter, sugar, and salt; beat until smooth. Add enough of the remaining flour to form a smooth and elastic dough.
2. Turn onto a floured surface; knead for 6 minutes. Place it in a greased bowl, turning once to grease top. Cover and let rise in a warm place for about 1 hour.
3. Punch your dough down and then turn it onto a floured surface. Divide the dough into 16 pieces and shape each into a ball. Place them two inches apart on greased baking sheets; cover and let it rise until it doubles for about 30 minutes.

4. Bake the dough at 350°C for about 40 minutes until golden brown, and then remove from pans to wire racks. Serve warm.

Nutrition Facts

Calories: 168

Fat: 2g

Cholesterol: 6mg

Sodium: 174mg

Carbohydrate: 32g

Protein: 4g

54. GLUTEN AND DAIRY-FREE CINNAMON RAISIN BREAD

Prep: 25 min

Bake: 45 min plus cooling

Ingredients

- ½ teaspoon baking soda
- 2 cups + 1 tablespoon gluten-free all-purpose baking flour
- 1 cup sugar, divided
- ½ cup canola oil
- 1 cup coconut milk
- 1 ½ teaspoons baking powder
- ¼ teaspoon salt
- 1 teaspoon vanilla extract
- 1 cup raisins
- 2 large eggs
- 3 teaspoons ground cinnamon
- Dairy-free spreadable margarine, optional

Preparation

1. Whisk flour, baking soda, baking powder, 3/4 cup sugar, and salt in a large bowl. Whisk coconut milk, eggs, oil, and vanilla in another bowl until blended. Add it to the flour mixture; stir just until moistened. Toss the raisins with remaining flour; fold into batter.

2. Transfer half of the batter to a greased 9x5-inch loaf pan. Combine the cinnamon and remaining sugar. Sprinkle half over batter—repeat layers. Cut through batter with a knife to swirl.
3. Preheat oven to 350°C. Bake for 45–50 minutes.
4. Cool in pans for 10 minutes before removing a wire rack to cool completely. If desired, serve with dairy-free margarine.

Nutrition Facts

Calories: 295

Fat: 14g

Cholesterol: 31mg

Sodium: 180mg

Carbohydrate: 42g

Protein: 4g

55. HAWAIIAN SWEET BREAD

Prep: 30 min

Rising Bake & Cooling: 30 min

Ingredients

- 1/2 cup warm water (110°C to 115°C)
- 8 cups all-purpose flour, divided
- 2 (1/4 ounce each) active dry yeast
- 1 cup whole milk
- 3/4 cup mashed potato flakes
- 2/3 cup sugar
- 1/2 cup butter, softened
- 1 teaspoon salt
- 2 teaspoons vanilla extract
- 1/2 teaspoon ground ginger
- 1 cup pineapple juice
- 3 large eggs, lightly beaten (room temperature)

Preparation

1. Dissolve yeast in warm water in a bowl. Let it stand until bubbles form on the surface for 5 min.

2. Meanwhile, heat butter until it melts in a small saucepan, then add pineapple juice and whole milk and gently heat until the mixture reaches 110°C–115°C.

3. Combine three cups of flour, potato flakes, ginger sugar, and salt in a large bowl. Add butter mixtures and yeast to dry ingredients, then beat until moistened. Add eggs and beat until smooth. Beat the mix in vanilla and stir in enough remaining flour to form a soft dough; a sticky dough will be formed.

4. Turn dough onto a floured surface; with floured hands, knead for 8-10 minutes until smooth and elastic, adding more flour to the surface and hands as needed. Place in a greased bowl and turn once to grease the top. Cover and let rise in a warm place until doubled for about 1 ¼ hours.

5. Punch your dough down and turn it onto a lightly floured surface. Divide it into thirds while shaping each into a ball. Place them in three greased 9-inch round baking pans lined with parchment; cover and let rise until it doubles in about 45 minutes.

6. Preheat oven to 350°C and bake for about 30-35 minutes until golden brown. The internal temperature of the loaves will reach 200°C. Cover it loosely with foil at the last 10 minutes of baking if needed to prevent tops from over-browning, then remove from pans to wire racks to cool.

Nutrition Facts

Calories: 146

Fat: 3g

Cholesterol: 25mg

Sodium: 103mg

Carbohydrate: 25g

Protein: 4g.

56. OATMEAL DINNER ROLLS

Prep: 40 min

Rising Bake: 20 min

Ingredients

- 2 cups water
- 1 cup quick-cooking oats
- 3 tablespoons butter
- 1/4-ounce active dry yeast
- 1/3 cup warm water (110° to 115°)
- 1/3 cup packed brown sugar
- 1 tablespoon sugar
- 1 ½ teaspoons salt
- 5 ¼ cups all-purpose flour

Preparation

1. Bring the water to a boil in a large saucepan, then add butter and oats —Cook and stir for 1 minute. Remove from the heat; cool to lukewarm.
2. In a large bowl, dissolve yeast in warm water. Add the oat mixture, sugars, salt, and 4 cups flour; beat until smooth. Add enough remaining flour to form a soft dough.
3. Turn onto a floured surface; knead until smooth and elastic, 6-8 minutes. Place in a greased bowl, turning once to grease top. Cover and let rise in a warm place until doubled, about 1 hour.
4. Punch dough down; allow to rest for 10 minutes. Shape into 18 balls. Place in two greased 9-in. round baking pans. Cover and let rise until doubled, about 45 minutes.
5. Preheat oven to 350°; bake rolls until golden brown, 20-25 minutes. Remove from pans to wire racks.

Nutrition Facts

Calories: 173

Fat: 3g

Sodium: 221mg

Carbohydrate: 33g

Protein: 4g

57. HERB BUTTERMILK DINNER ROLLS

Prep: 20 min

Rising Bake: 25 min

Ingredients

- 1/4-ounce active dry yeast
- 1/4 cup warm water
- 3/4 cup warm buttermilk
- 4 tablespoons butter, melted, divided
- 2 tablespoons sugar
- 1-1/2 teaspoons salt
- 1/2 teaspoon dried basil
- 1/2 teaspoon dried marjoram
- 1/2 teaspoon dried thyme
- 1/4 teaspoon baking soda
- 1 large egg, room temperature
- 3 ¼ cups all-purpose flour

Preparation

1. Dissolve yeast in warm water. Add buttermilk, 2 tablespoons butter, and the next 7 ingredients. Stir in 2 cups flour. Beat until smooth. Stir in enough remaining flour to form a soft dough, which will be sticky.
2. Turn onto a heavily floured surface; knead until smooth and elastic, 6–8 minutes. Place in a greased bowl, turning once to grease top. Cover and let rise in a warm place until doubled, about 75 minutes.
3. Punch dough down. Turn onto a lightly floured surface; divide into 4 portions. Divide each portion into 6 pieces; shape each piece into a ball—place in a greased 13x9-inch baking pan. Cover and let rise for about 50 minutes until doubled.
4. Preheat oven to 375°. Bake the rolls for 25–30 minutes, until golden brown. Cool them 5 minutes before removing them from the pan to a wire rack. Brush with remaining butter.

Nutrition Facts

Calories: 78

Fat: 2g

Cholesterol: 14mg

Sodium: 186mg

Carbohydrate: 12g

Protein: 2g

58. PARMESAN SCONES

Total Time: 25 min

Ingredients

- 2 cups finely chopped onions
- 2 tablespoons olive oil
- 6 garlic cloves, minced
- 4 cups all-purpose flour
- 2 cups grated Parmesan cheese
- 4 teaspoons baking powder
- 1 teaspoon salt
- 2 cups heavy whipping cream
- Additional grated Parmesan cheese, optional

Preparation

1. In a large skillet, sauté onions in oil until tender. Add garlic to sauté 1 minute longer.
2. Combine the flour, cheese, baking powder, and salt in a large bowl. Stir in cream just until moistened. Stir in onion mixture.
3. Turn onto a floured surface and knead about ten times. Divide dough in half. Pat each portion into a 6-in. circle. Cut each circle into six wedges—separate wedges and place them on a greased baking sheet.
4. Bake at 400°C for 12-15 minutes or until light golden brown. If desired, sprinkle with additional cheese in the last 5 minutes of baking. Serve warm.

Nutrition Facts

Calories: 378

Fat: 21g

Cholesterol: 66mg

Sodium: 551mg

Carbohydrate: 36g

Protein: 11g

59. COUNTRY CRUST SOURDOUGH BREAD

Prep: 20 min.

Rising Bake: 30 min

Ingredients

- 6 ½ cups all-purpose flour
- 1 cup Sourdough Starter
- 2 (1/4 ounce each) active dry yeast
- 1/4 cup vegetable oil
- 2 large eggs (room temperature)
- 1 ¼ cups warm water (110°C to 150°C)
- 1/4 cup sugar
- 1 teaspoon salt
- Melted butter

Preparation

1. Dissolve yeast in warm water in a large bowl. Add the sourdough starter, 3 cups flour, eggs, oil, sugar, and salt. Beat them until smooth and stir in enough remaining flour to form a soft dough.
2. Turn the dough onto a floured surface and knead for 8 minutes until it is smooth and elastic. Place it in a greased bowl and turn it once to grease top; cover and let it proof for 60 min in a warm place.
3. Punch the dough down and turn it onto a lightly floured surface. Divide it into half and then shape it into loaves—place in 2 greased 8x4-inch loaf pans; cover it and let rise for about 45 minutes until it doubles.
4. Bake at 375°C for 35 minutes or until golden brown. Remove the bread from pans to wire racks to cool. Brush with butter.

Nutrition Facts

Calories: 113

Fat: 2g

Cholesterol: 12mg

Sodium: 79mg

Carbohydrate: 20g

Protein: 3g

Prep time: 40 min

Rising bake time: 20 min

Ingredients

- 1/2 cup sugar
- 1/4-ounce active dry yeast
- 1 cup warm whole milk (110° C to 115°C)
- 1/3 cup butter, melted
- 2 large eggs, room temperature
- 1 teaspoon salt
- 4 ½ cups all-purpose flour

Filling

- 2 tablespoons ground cinnamon
- 3/4 cup packed brown sugar
- 1/4 cup butter, melted, divided

Frosting

- 1 ½ cups confectioners' sugar
- 1/2 cup butter, softened
- 1/2 teaspoon vanilla extract

- 1/4 cup cream cheese, softened
- 1/8 teaspoon salt

Preparation

1. Dissolve the yeast in warm milk in another bowl. Combine two cups flour, butter, eggs, sugar, salt, and yeast mixture; beat on medium speed until smooth. Stir in enough remaining flour to form a soft dough
2. Turn dough onto a floured surface; knead until smooth and elastic, 6–8 minutes. Place in a greased bowl, turning once to grease the top. Cover and let rise in a warm place until doubled, about 1 hour.
3. Mix brown sugar and cinnamon. Punch down dough; divide in half. On a lightly floured surface, roll one portion into an 11x8-inch rectangle. Brush with two tablespoons butter; sprinkle with half the brown sugar mixture to within 1/2 inch of edges. Roll up jelly-roll style, starting with a long side; pinch seam to seal. Cut into eight slices; place in a greased 13x9-inch pan, cut side down. Cover with a kitchen towel. Repeat with remaining dough and filling. Let it rise for 60 min in a warm. place
4. Preheat oven to 350°C and bake for 25 minutes until golden brown. Cool on wire racks.
5. For frosting, beat butter, cream cheese, vanilla, and salt until blended; gradually beat in confectioners' sugar. Spread over tops. Refrigerate leftovers.

Nutrition Facts

Calories: 364

Fat: 15g

Cholesterol: 66mg

Sodium: 323mg

Carbohydrate: 53g

Protein: 5g

61. PERFECT DINNER ROLLS

Prep: 30 min

Rising Bake: 15 min

Ingredients

- 1 tablespoon active dry yeast
- 2 ¼ cups warm water (110° to 115°)
- 1/3 cup sugar
- 1/3 cup shortening
- 1/4 cup powdered non-dairy creamer
- 2 ¼ teaspoons salt
- 7 cups bread flour

Preparation

1. In a large bowl, dissolve yeast in warm water. Add the sugar, shortening, creamer, salt, and 5 cups flour. Beat until smooth. Stir in enough remaining flour to form a soft dough (dough will be sticky).
2. Turn onto a floured surface; knead until smooth and elastic, 6-8 minutes—place in a bowl coated with cooking spray, turning once to coat the top. Cover and let rise in a warm place until doubled, about 1 hour.
3. Punch the dough down; turn it onto a lightly floured surface. Divide it into 24 pieces. Shape each into a roll. Place them 2 inches apart and coat with cooking spray. Cover and let rise for about 30 minutes until it doubles.
4. Meanwhile, preheat the oven to 350°. Bake rolls until lightly browned, 12-15 minutes. Remove from pans to wire racks.

Nutrition Facts

Calories: 142

Fat: 3g

Sodium: 222mg

Carbohydrate: 25g

Protein: 4g

62. GLUTEN-FREE SANDWICH BREAD

Prep: 20 min

Rising bake: 30 min

Ingredients

- 2 tablespoons sugar
- 1 tablespoon active dry yeast
- 3 tablespoons canola oil
- 1 cup warm fat-free milk (110° to 115°C)
- 1 teaspoon cider vinegar
- 2 ½ cups gluten-free all-purpose baking flour
- 2 ½ teaspoons xanthan gum
- 1/2 teaspoon salt
- 1 teaspoon unflavored gelatin
- 2 large eggs, room temperature

Preparation

1. Grease a 9x5-inch loaf pan; sprinkle with gluten-free flour; set aside.
2. Dissolve the yeast and sugar in warm milk in a small bowl. Combine the eggs, vinegar, oil, and yeast mixture in a stand mixer with a paddle attachment. Gradually beat in the flour, gelatin, salt, and xanthan gum. Beat on low speed for 1 minute. Beat on medium for 2 minutes. Your dough will be softer than yeast bread dough with gluten.
3. Transfer to the prepared pan—smooth the top with a wet spatula. Cover with a towel; let rise for 25 minutes in a warm place until dough reaches the top of the pan.
4. Preheat oven to 375°C and bake for 20 minutes; cover loosely with foil. Bake until golden brown for 10-15 minutes longer.
5. Remove it from the pan; place it on a wire rack to cool.

Nutrition Facts

Calories: 110

Fat: 4g

Cholesterol: 27mg

Sodium: 95mg

Carbohydrate: 17g

Protein: 4g

Prep: 20 min

Bake: 50 min

Ingredients

- 1 cup all-purpose flour
- 1 cup whole wheat flour
- 1/2 cup sugar
- 1 ½ teaspoon ground cinnamon, divided
- 1 teaspoon baking soda
- 1/2 teaspoon salt
- 1/2 teaspoon baking powder
- 1/4 teaspoon ground nutmeg
- 2 large eggs, room temperature
- 1 ¼ cups unsweetened applesauce
- 1/4 cup canola oil
- 3 tablespoons 2% milk
- 1/4 cup packed brown sugar

Preparation

1. Preheat oven to 350°. Combine the flour, sugar, 1 teaspoon cinnamon, baking soda, salt, baking powder, and nutmeg in a large bowl. Whisk the eggs, applesauce, oil, and milk in a small bowl. Stir into dry ingredients just until moistened.
2. Transfer to a greased 9x5-inch loaf pan. Combine the remaining 1/2 teaspoon cinnamon and brown sugar; sprinkle over the top.
3. Bake for about 60 minutes. Cool for 10 minutes, then remove it to a wire rack from the pan.

Nutrition Facts

Calories:142

Fat: 4g

Cholesterol: 23mg

Sodium: 179mg

Carbohydrate: 24g

Protein: 3g

64. STICKY BUNS

Prep: 30 min

Rising Bake: 20 min

Ingredients

- 2 teaspoons active dry yeast
- 1 ¼ cups warm water (110° to 115°)
- 3 tablespoons butter, softened
- 3 tablespoons sugar
- 2 tablespoons nonfat dry milk powder
- 1 teaspoon salt
- 3 ¾ cups bread flour

Sauce

- 1/2 cup packed brown sugar
- 1/4 cup butter, cubed
- 1/4 cup corn syrup
- 1/2 cup chopped pecans

Filling

- 1/3 cup butter, softened
- 1 tablespoon sugar
- 1 teaspoon ground cinnamon

Preparation

1. Dissolve yeast in water. Add butter, sugar, milk powder, and salt, then beat in 2 cups flour on low for 3 minutes. Stir in enough remaining flour to form a soft dough.
2. Turn onto a floured surface; knead until smooth and elastic, 6–8 minutes. Place dough in a greased bowl, turning once to grease top. Cover and let rise in a warm place until doubled, about 1 hour.
3. Meanwhile, in a small saucepan, make a sauce by combining butter, corn syrup, and brown sugar. Cook over medium heat until the sugar dissolves. Stir in pecans. Pour into a greased 13x9-inch baking dish.
4. Punch it down; turn it onto a floured surface, roll it into a 16x10-inch rectangle. Make the filling by combining butter, sugar, and cinnamon; spread to within 3/4 in. of edges. Roll up jelly-roll style, starting with a long side; pinch seam to seal. Cut into 12 slices; place slices cut side down over sauce. Cover with a kitchen towel; let rise in a warm place until doubled, about 45 minutes.
5. Preheat oven to 375°. Bake until golden brown, 20-25 minutes. Cool 3 minutes before inverting onto a serving platter.

Nutrition Facts

Calories: 314

Fat: 15g

Cholesterol: 32mg

Sodium: 334mg

Carbohydrate: 42g

Protein: 5g

65. BAKER'S DOZEN YEAST ROLLS

Total time: 1 hour

Ingredients

- 3/4 cup warm water (at 120° to 130℃)
- 2 ½ cups all-purpose flour
- 1/4 ounce quick-rise yeast
- 1/8 teaspoon garlic salt
- 2 tablespoons sugar
- 2 tablespoons + 4 teaspoons butter, melted, divided
- 3/4 cup shredded sharp cheddar cheese
- 1/2 teaspoon salt
- 2 teaspoons honey

Preparation

1. Combine 1 ½ cups flour, sugar, yeast, and salt in a large bowl. Add water and 2 tablespoons butter; beat on medium speed for 3 minutes or until smooth. Stir in cheese and enough remaining flour to form a soft dough.
2. Turn onto a lightly floured surface; knead until smooth and elastic, about 4–6 minutes. Cover and let rest for 10 minutes. Divide into 13 pieces. Shape each into a ball. Place in a greased 9-in. round baking pan. Cover and let rise in a warm place until doubled, about 30 minutes.
3. Preheat oven to 375°. Bake rolls 11-14 minutes or until lightly browned. Combine honey, garlic salt, and remaining butter; brush over rolls. Remove from pan to wire rack.

Nutrition Facts

Calories: 131

Fat: 5g

Cholesterol: 15mg

Sodium: 169mg

Carbohydrate: 18g

Protein: 4g

66. CRESCENT DINNER ROLLS

Prep: 40 min

Rising bake: 10 min

Ingredients

- 1/4 cup warm water (at 110° to 115°C)
- 1 tablespoon plus 1/2 cup sugar, divided
- 3/4 cup warm milk (at 110° to 115°C)
- 3 large eggs, room temperature, lightly beaten
- 1/4-ounce active dry yeast
- 1/2 cup butter, softened
- 1 teaspoon salt
- 5 ½ cups all-purpose flour
- Melted butter

Preparation

1. dissolve yeast in warm water in a large bowl and then add one tablespoon sugar; let stand for 5 minutes. Add the milk, eggs, butter, salt, and remaining sugar. Stir in enough flour to form a stiff dough. Turn onto a floured surface; knead until smooth and elastic, 6-8 minutes. Place in a greased bowl, turning once to grease top. Cover and let rise in a warm place until doubled for about 1 ½ hours.
2. Punch dough down. Divide into thirds. Roll each into a 12-inch circle, then cut each circle into eight wedges. Brush with melted butter; roll up wedges from the wide end and place, pointed end down, 2 in. apart on greased baking sheets. Cover and let rise in a warm place until doubled, about 30 minutes. Bake for 10-12 minutes at 375° or until golden brown. Remove from pans to wire racks.

Nutrition Facts

Calories: 161

Fat: 5g

Cholesterol: 38mg

Sodium: 149mg

Carbohydrate: 25g

Protein: 4g

67. HONEY CORNBREAD

Total Time: 30 min

Ingredients

- 1 cup all-purpose flour
- 1 cup yellow cornmeal
- 1/4 cup sugar
- 3 teaspoons baking powder
- 1/2 teaspoon salt
- 2 large eggs, room temperature
- 1 cup heavy whipping cream
- 1/4 cup canola oil
- 1/4 cup honey

Preparation

1. Combine flour, cornmeal, sugar, baking powder, and salt in a bowl. Beat the eggs in a small bowl, add oil, honey, and cream, and beat well. Stir into the dry ingredients until it moistens. Pour into a greased 9-inch square baking pan.
2. Preheat oven to 400°C. Bake for 25 minutes. Serve warm.

Nutrition Facts

Calories: 318

Fat: 17g

Cholesterol: 83mg

Sodium: 290mg

Carbohydrate: 37g

Protein: 5g

68. SAVOURY PUMPKIN BREAD

Prep: 30 min

Bake: 65 min

Ingredients

- 3 tablespoons butter
- 1 cup chopped shelled pistachios
- 1/2 teaspoon ground turmeric
- 1/2 teaspoon ground cumin
- 1/4 teaspoon cayenne pepper

Batter

- 2/3 cup butter, softened
- 2 2/3 cups sugar
- 4 large eggs, room temperature
- 15 ounces pumpkin
- 2/3 cup water
- 3 ½ cups self-rising flour
- 1 teaspoon pumpkin pie spice

Preparation

1. Melt the softened butter over medium heat in a saucepan. Cook until butter is golden brown for 7 minutes; keep stirring constantly. Remove it from heat and stir in pistachios, turmeric, cumin, and cayenne. Let cool.
2. In a large bowl, beat 2/3 cup butter and sugar until crumbly for the batter and add an egg at a time while beating each well after each addition. Beat in pumpkin and water. Whisk flour and pie spice in another bowl; add to butter mixture just until moistened. Fold in pistachio mixture.
3. Preheat oven to 350°C. Transfer to two greased 9x5-inch loaf pans. Bake for 70 minutes until a toothpick inserted in the center comes out clean,
4. Cool in pans for 10 minutes before moving to wire rack to cool completely.

Nutrition Facts

Calories: 193

Fat: 7g

Cholesterol: 36mg

Sodium: 228mg

Carbohydrate: 29g

Protein: 3g

69. EASY MILK BREAD ROLLS

Preparation time: 30 minutes

Cook time: 25 minutes

Resting time: 2 hours

Total time: 2 hours 55 minutes

Servings: 9 rolls

Ingredients

- 300g bread flour
- 7g yeast
- 30g sugar
- 5g salt
- 1/2 cup whole milk, extra for brushing onto the bread
- ¼ cup sweetened condensed milk
- 4 tablespoons unsalted butter, melted
- 1 large egg

Preparation

First rise

1. Add the milk into a small bowl. Warm to approximately 38°C for about 30 seconds in the microwave. Add the active dry yeast and a pinch of sugar and let it sit for 5 minutes; the yeast will activate.
2. As the yeast activates, add the rest of the ingredients into your mixer bowl.
3. Once the yeast is activated, pour it into the mixer bowl and mix with a spatula until the dough just comes together. Cover with plastic wrap. Let rest for 20 minutes.
4. Install the dough hook on your mixer if using KitchenAid, then Start at low speed, then gradually increase the speed by setting 8 out of 10. Knead for 12 minutes; the dough will be very smooth. Stop the mixer in the middle and then scrape the dough from the sides of the bowl. Test your dough by pulling a piece of it using both of your hands; the dough should stretch to very thin and translucent sheets. It should be wet and a bit sticky.
5. Grease your bowl with a thin layer of oil and place your dough into it. Cover the dough with plastic wrap. Let it rise; your dough will double in size in about one hour.

Second rise

1. Line a 23cm by 23cm baking pan parchment, punch the air out of the dough and then transfer your dough onto a lightly oiled working surface.
2. Divide the dough into nine even pieces by cutting it into three even strips. Divide each strip into three small pieces; each piece of dough should weigh about 68 to 70g.
3. Shape it one piece at a time. Tuck your dough onto itself by pinching it from all sides into the center using your fingers to create a round shape. Roll it in a circular motion with your palm against the table until it forms a round ball. Place your dough balls onto the parchment paper, evenly spaced, in a 3-by-3 array.
4. Cover the baking pan with plastic wrap. Let rest for another 35 to 45 minutes until the size has doubled.

Baking

1. Preheat the oven to 176° C while resting the shaped bread rolls.
2. Before you start baking, gently brush a thin layer of milk onto the tops of the bread rolls. Proceed with baking the milk bread rolls on the middle rack for about 25 minutes. The top will turn golden brown.
3. Allow your dough to rest in the pan for 5 minutes. Transfer it onto a cooling rack.
4. Serve warm

Nutrition Facts

Calories: 226kcal

Carbohydrates: 34.7g

Protein: 5.6g

Fat: 7.3g

Cholesterol: 36mg

Sodium: 279mg

Potassium: 115mg

Fiber: 1.1g

70. SWEET POTATO SPICE BREAD

Prep: 15 min

Bake: 25 min

Ingredients

- 1 cup all-purpose flour
- 1/3 cup mashed sweet potato
- 2 tablespoons of molasses
- 3 tablespoons canola oil
- 1/8 teaspoonful salt
- 1 large egg
- 1/3 cup honey
- 1 ½ teaspoons of baking powder
- 1/3 cup chopped walnuts
- ¼ teaspoonful each ground cinnamon, allspice, and nutmeg

Preparation

1. Combine the flour, baking powder, spices, and salt in a small bowl. Whisk the egg, honey, sweet potato, oil, and molasses in another small bowl. Stir into dry ingredients and fold in walnuts.
2. Transfer to two greased 5 ¾ x3x2 inch loaf pans. Bake at 325°C for 30 minutes or until a toothpick inserted in the center comes out clean.
3. Cool for them for 10 minutes before removing from pans to wire racks.

Nutrition Facts

Calories: 142

Fat: 6g

Cholesterol: 18mg

Sodium: 85mg

Carbohydrate: 20g

Protein: 3g

71. GLUTEN-FREE BANANA BREAD

Prep: 20 min

Bake: 45 min

Ingredients

- 2 cups gluten-free all-purpose baking flour
- 1 teaspoon baking soda
- 1/4 teaspoon salt
- 4 large eggs, room temperature
- 2 cups mashed ripe bananas
- 1 cup sugar
- 1/2 cup unsweetened applesauce
- 1/3 cup canola oil
- 1 teaspoon vanilla extract
- 1/2 cup chopped walnuts

Preparation

1. combine flour, baking soda, and salt in a large bowl. Whisk eggs, bananas, sugar, applesauce, oil, and vanilla in a small bowl. Stir into dry ingredients just until moistened.
2. Transfer to 2 greased 8x4-inch loaf pans. Sprinkle with walnuts.
3. Preheat oven to 350°C. Bake for about 45-55 minutes or until a toothpick inserted in the center comes out clean. Cool for 10 minutes before removing from pans to wire racks.

Nutrition Facts

Calories: 140

Fat: 6g

Cholesterol: l35mg

Sodium: 89mg

Carbohydrate: 21g

Protein: 3g

72. BAKED SCALLION BREAD

Prep time: 30 mins

Cook time: 35 mins

Rest time: 2 hours

Equipment

- Medium mixing bowl
- 9 x 5-inch baking tin
- Rolling pin

Ingredients

Tangzhong (makes 1/2 cup)

- 3 tablespoons of bread flour
- 1/4 cup water
- 1/4 cup milk

Dough

- 1/2 cup tangzhong
- 1/2 cup milk, lukewarm
- 3 tablespoon granulated sugar
- 2 tsp. instant or active dry yeast
- 2 ½ cup bread flour
- 1 tsp. salt
- 1 egg
- 4 tablespoon unsalted butter, room temperature

Filling

- ¼ tsp. salt
- 2 tablespoon softened butter
- 1 bunch scallions, chopped

Topping

- white sesame seeds
- 2 tablespoon milk

Preparation

Make tangzhong

1. Whisk together bread flour, water, and milk until smooth in a small skillet. Bring to simmer over medium-low heat, frequently whisking, until mixture has thickened but is still pourable. It should take about 10 minutes (Your whisk should leave a mark when dragged along the bottom of the pan).
2. Pour into a bowl and then cover the surface with plastic wrap; this prevents a film from foaming and allows it to cool to room temperature.

Dough

1. Mix warm milk, yeast, and sugar. Set aside for about 5 minutes; the milk at this point should feel comfortably warm to the touch but not hot so that it does not kill your yeast. If there is no sign of foaming activity, the yeast may be dead.
2. Add flour, tangzhong, egg, and salt to the milk and yeast mixture. Using a stand mixer fitted with a dough hook attachment, mix on low speed until a shaggy dough forms. Slowly add in softened butter pieces while the mixer runs at medium-low speed. Continue mixing for 15 minutes until the dough is smooth.
3. Shape them into a ball. Place into a lightly greased mixing bowl. Cover with plastic wrap. Let rise for about 50 minutes until roughly doubled in size.
4. Grease a baking tin, set it aside, and turn the dough onto a lightly floured surface. Knead a few times.
5. Roll the dough you made into a 10 x 15-inch rectangle and spread the surface of the dough with 1 tablespoon of vegetable shortening. Sprinkle with 1/2 of the chopped scallions and roll the dough up so that you have a 15-inch tube. Then, coil the tube to round dough pieces swirled like a snail shell.
6. Repeat the layering process by rolling out this piece of dough into a 10 x 15-inch rectangle. Spread the surface of the dough with 1 tablespoon of vegetable shortening. Sprinkle with 1/4 teaspoon of salt and the remaining chopped scallions; a few scallions will be left for garnishing the top. Roll the dough up so that you have a 15-inch tube. Using a knife, cut the tube in half length-wise. Turn the inside of the tube up and twist the two pieces over each other. Tuck the ends of the braid underneath and place the dough into your prepared baking tin.
7. Preheat oven to 350 F and allow the loaf to proof for 60 minutes. Brush the top of the loaf with milk and sprinkle with leftover scallions and sesame seeds.
8. Place the dough in the lower third of the oven and bake for 35 minutes; this makes it change color into golden brown and produce a hollow sound when tapped.
9. Remove it from the oven. Let the bread cool for approximately 15 minutes in the tin. Remove from tin and place on a wire cooling rack to finish cooling.

Nutrition Facts

Calories: 130

Total Fat: 4g

Sodium: 260mg

Total Carbohydrate: 19g

Dietary Fiber: 1g

Total Sugars: 1g

Protein: 3g

73. 40-MINUTE HAMBURGER BUNS

Prep: 20 min

Resting Bake: 10 min

Ingredients

- 3 ½ cups all-purpose flour
- 1 cup + 2 tablespoons warm water (110° to 115°C)
- 1/3 cup vegetable oil
- 2 tablespoons active dry yeast
- 1 teaspoon salt
- 1/4 cup sugar
- 1 large egg, room temperature

Preparation

1. In a large bowl, dissolve yeast in warm water. Add oil and sugar; let stand for 5 minutes. Add the egg, salt, and enough flour to form a soft dough.
2. Turn onto a floured surface; knead until smooth and elastic, 3-5 minutes. Do not let rise. Divide into 12 pieces; shape each into a ball. Place 3 in. apart on greased baking sheets. Cover and let rest for 10 minutes.
3. Preheat oven to 425°C. Bake for 12 minutes; Remove from pan and place on wire racks to cool for 5 minutes.

Nutrition Facts

Calories: 195

Fat: 7g

Cholesterol: 18mg

Sodium: 204mg

Carbohydrate: 29g

Protein: 5g

74. MILK BREAD

Prep time: 20 minutes

Cook time: 40 minutes

Inactive prep (rising) time: 3 hours

Total time: 4 hours

Ingredients

- 3 tablespoons of granulated sugar
- 9 ounces' bread flour
- 6 ¾ to 9 ounces' all-purpose flour
- 2 ¼ teaspoon instant yeast
- 1 teaspoon salt
- 1 cup whole milk
- 2 ½ ounces unsalted butter melted
- 1 large egg lightly beaten
- 1 tablespoon heavy cream or milk for brushing

Preparation

1. Add bread flour, yeast, sugar, salt, and 6 ¾ ounces of all-purpose flour to the bowl of a stand mixer and whisk together. Slowly add butter, milk, and egg while the machine runs on medium-low or low speed. Gradually add as much of the remaining all-purpose flour as needed until the dough is moist but not sticky.
2. Knead for about 10 minutes using medium speed; the dough will be smooth. Transfer your dough to an oiled bowl and then turn over once to coat with oil. Cover it loosely with plastic. Let rise in a warm place; it will double in volume in about 1–1.5 hours.
3. Punch down the knead briefly. Refrigerate for 30 minutes. Form into a loaf, place in greased 8 1/2 x 4 ½ loaf pan. Cover loosely with plastic wrap. Let rise until doubled, 1 to 1.5 hours.
4. Preheat the oven to about 375 F. Brush the top of the loaf with cream. Bake for 35 minutes; the top will be golden, and the bottom sounds hollow when tapped. Cool completely on a wire rack.

Nutrition Facts

Calories: 324kcal

Carbohydrates: 47g

Protein: 10g

Fat: 9g

Cholesterol: 43mg

Sodium: 302mg

Potassium: 97mg

Fiber: 2g

75. SWEET POTATO MILK BREAD DOUGH

Yield: Makes 3 ½ pounds of dough

Ingredients

- 1 cup whole milk, warmed
- 2 1/4 teaspoons active dry yeast
- 2 large eggs
- 1 ½ cups sweet potato puree from orange-fleshed sweet potatoes
- 5 tablespoons sugar 1 tablespoon kosher salt
- 4 tablespoons unsalted butter, melted
- 6 cups all-purpose flour; more may be required for dusting

Preparation

1. Gently stir together the yeast, one cup of warm milk, and a tablespoon of the sugar in a large bowl or bowl of a stand mixer. Let stand until the mixture becomes foamy for about 5 minutes.
2. Add the sweet potato puree, the remaining four tablespoons of sugar, butter, eggs, and salt to the yeast mixture.
3. Fit your machine with the hook attachment and mix the ingredients at low speed until smooth, about a minute. With the machine running, add the flour, a cup at a time. When all the flour has been added, increase the speed from low to medium. Knead for 10 minutes; the dough will be silky smooth, soft, and a little sticky.
4. Alternatively, when making the dough by hand, whisk the remaining four tablespoons of sugar, sweet potato, eggs, salt, and butter into the yeast mixture to form a smooth mixture. Place the flour in a large bowl, make a well in the center, and pour the sweet potato mixture into the well you created. Mix it with the flour using a wooden spoon, stirring until the dough is too stiff to mix with the spoon, and then lightly butter your hands. Knead the dough for about 10 minutes in the bowl until smooth.
5. Brush your large, clean bowl with some melted butter. Shape the dough into a ball, set it in the bowl, and seam-side down; cover the bowl loosely with plastic wrap and let rise in a warm spot until it doubles in volume for an hour. Punch the dough down and use it immediately.

Nutrition Facts

Calories: 72

Total Fat: 1.53g

Cholesterol: 14mg

Sodium: 237mg

Total Carbohydrate: 12.48g

Sugars: 1.84g

Protein: 1.97g

Calcium: 5mg

Iron: 0.77mg

Potassium: 40mg

76. HOMEMADE GLUTEN-FREE BREAD

Prep time10 minutes

Cook time: 2 hours 30 minutes

Total time: 2 hours 40 minutes

Ingredients

- 1 teaspoon apple cider vinegar
- 1 ½ cups warm milk, dairy-free use cashew, coconut milk, or almond
- ¼ cup unsalted butter
- ½ cup honey
- 1 teaspoon salt
- 1 ½ teaspoons xanthan gum, leave it out if your flour already has it
- 2 eggs, beaten
- 3 cups all-purpose gluten-free flour
- 1 ¾ teaspoons rapid yeast/instant yeast

Preparation

1. Add all the wet ingredients above to the bread-baking pan.
2. Warm the milk and melt butter, then add the milk and butter to a large glass measuring cup and heat in the microwave. Pour the melted butter and warm milk into the bread-baking pan.
3. Pour the honey, beaten eggs, and lastly, apple cider vinegar into the bread-baking pan. Add the dry ingredients.
4. Add salt, flour, and xanthan gum (leave out if your flour already has it) to the bread baking pan.
5. The last step is to add your yeast. First, make a tiny hole with your finger in the flour. Pour the yeast into the hole.
6. Start the bread machine, set it to a gluten-free setting. While the bread machine is mixing, go in and scrape the sides down into the batter with a spatula resulting in a dough similar to the cake batter.
7. Cool before slicing. Enjoy!

Nutrition Facts

Calories: 212kcal

Carbohydrates: 35g

Protein: 5g

Fat: 6g

Cholesterol: 40mg

Sodium: 263mg

Potassium: 74mg

Fiber: 3g

Sugar: 14g

Calcium: 61mg

Iron: 1.3mg

77. NO-KNEAD CASSEROLE BREAD

Prep: 15 min

Rising bake: 45 min

Ingredients

- 1/4 cup finely chopped onion
- 1 ½ teaspoons salt
- 2 packages (1/4 ounce each) quick-rise yeast
- 1/2 teaspoon pepper
- 3/4 cup + 2 tablespoons shredded cheddar cheese, divided
- 5 ½ cups all-purpose flour
- 2 tablespoons sugar
- 2 tablespoons butter, cubed
- 2 cups water

Preparation

1. Mix 2 ½ cups flour, yeast, salt, sugar, and pepper in a large bowl. Heat water and butter to 120°-130°C in a small saucepan and stir into dry ingredients. Stir in onion, 3/4 cup cheese, and remaining flour. A soft dough will be formed. Cover it with plastic wrap. Let rest for 10 minutes.
2. Shape it into a ball; place it in a greased 2-qt. round baking dish. Cover it with a kitchen towel and let rise for about 20 minutes in a warm place until it doubles.
3. Preheat oven to 350°.Bake for 40-45 minutes; the dough will turn golden brown. Sprinkle it with the remaining cheese and bake for 5 minutes longer or until cheese is melted.
4. Cool in a baking dish 5 minutes before removing a wire rack to cool.

Nutrition Facts

Calories: 204

Fat: 4g

Cholesterol: 10mg

Sodium: 272mg

Carbohydrate: 35g

Protein: 6g

Prep time: 25 minutes

Cook time: 24 minutes

Rising time: 6 hours

Total time: 49 minutes

Ingredients

- ½ cup heavy cream
- ½ cup whole milk
- ¼ cup granulated sugar
- 1 teaspoon active dry yeast
- ¾ tsp. kosher salt
- 2 cup all-purpose flour plus 2 tablespoons (reserved)
- Extra flour for rolling

Egg wash

- 1 whole egg
- 1 tablespoon whole milk

Preparation

1. Add milk and cream to a small saucepan and bring to a simmer; turn off the heat. Transfer to a stand mixer-mixing bowl. In the hot milk mixture, dissolve the sugar using a whisk. Let it cool to below 110°F.
2. Sprinkle the active dry yeast over the liquid surface. Let it bloom for 15 minutes; the mixture should puff up.
3. Add two cups of flour and salt to the liquid mixture. Knead with the dough hook on speed two until the dough comes together.
4. Add the reserved flour; if the dough is too wet, one tablespoon at a time. Continue to knead; the dough should still be wet but not too tacky.
5. Grease a large bowl with cooking spray. Dump it onto a lightly floured surface or countertop. Knead into a ball.
6. Place the dough into the prepared bowl. Let it rise a warm for about 3 hours until at least double in size. Dump your dough on a lightly floured countertop, divide it into eight equal portions and shape it into balls.
7. Grease a loaf pan and then line the bottom with a piece of parchment paper. Allow the excess to hang over the sides.
8. Arrange the dough balls in the loaf pan and let them rise in a warm place for 2.5 hours until double or triple in size.
9. Beat an egg with a tablespoon of whole milk to make an egg wash, then lightly brush the risen dough with egg wash.
10. Preheat the oven to 350°F and bake the dough for 24 minutes; the top will be golden brown

Nutrition Facts

Calories: 124.9

Total fat: 2.2g

Cholesterol: 5.0mg

Protein: 3.5g

Potassium: 67.0mg

Total Carbohydrate: 22.2g

Sodium: 202.7mg

Sugars: 2.7g

79. GOLDEN HONEY PAN ROLLS

Prep: 35 min

Rising bake: 20 min

Ingredients

- 1 large egg yolk, room temperature
- 1 cup warm 2% milk (at 70°C to 80°C)
- 2 tablespoons honey
- 1 large egg, room temperature
- 1/2 cup canola oil
- 2-1/4 teaspoons active dry yeast
- 1-1/2 teaspoons salt
- 3-1/2 cups bread flour

Glaze

- 1/3 cup sugar
- 1 tablespoon honey
- 2 tablespoons butter, melted
- 1 large egg white

Preparation

1. Place the first eight ingredients in the bread machine pan in the order suggested by the manufacturer. Remember to check the dough after 5 minutes of mixing; then add about 1 to 2 tablespoons of water or flour if necessary.
2. When the cycle is completed, turn dough onto a lightly floured surface. Punch down; cover, and let rest for 10 minutes. Divide into 24 pieces; shape each into a ball. Place 12 balls each in 2 greased 8-in. square baking pans. Cover and let rise in a warm place until doubled, about 30 minutes.

For the glaze

1. Combine butter, honey, sugar, and egg white; drizzle the mixture over the dough. Bake for about 20–25 minutes at 350°C. Brush with additional honey if desired.

Nutrition Facts

Calories: 139

Fat: 6g

Cholesterol: 22mg

Sodium: 168mg

Carbohydrate: 18g

Protein: 3g

80. EASY BANANA NUT BREAD

Prep: 10 min

Bake: 40 min

Ingredients

- 1 package yellow cake mix (regular size)
- 1 egg
- 1/2 cup 2% milk
- 1 cup mashed ripe bananas (2 medium size)
- 1/2 cup chopped pecans

Preparation

1. combine the cake mix, milk, and an egg in a large bowl. Add bananas, then beat on medium speed for 2 minutes. Stir in pecans.
2. Pour into two greased 8x4-inch loaf pans. Bake at 350°C for about 40-45 minutes until a toothpick is inserted in the center comes out clean. Cool for 10 minutes before removing from pans to wire racks to cool completely.

Nutrition Facts

Calories:117

Fat: 4g

Cholesterol: 9mg

Sodium: 145mg

Carbohydrate: 20g

Protein: 1g

81. MILK-AND-HONEY WHITE BREAD

Ingredients

- 8 ½ cups all-purpose flour
- 2 - 1/4-ounce active dry yeast packets
- 2 ½ cups warm whole milk (110°C to 115°C)
- 1/3 cup honey
- 2 teaspoons salt
- 1/4 cup butter, melted

Preparation

1. Dissolve the yeast in warm milk in a large bowl. Add butter, honey, salt, and 5 cups flour, and then beat until smooth while adding enough remaining flour to form a soft dough.
2. Turn onto a floured board and knead for 7 minutes; the dough formed will be smooth and elastic. Place in a greased bowl, turning once to grease top; cover and let rise for about an hour in a warm place.
3. Punch dough down and shape it into two loaves. Place in greased 9x5-inch loaf pans; cover and let it rise for about 30 minutes until it doubles.
4. Bake at 375°C until golden brown, 35 minutes. Cover loosely with foil if tops brown too quickly. Remove the bread from the pans.
5. Cool it on wire racks and serve.

Nutrition Facts

Calories: 149

Fat: 2g

Cholesterol: 6mg

Sodium: 172mg

Carbohydrate: 28g

Protein: 4g

82. HONEY-OAT PAN ROLLS

Prep: 45 min

Rising Bake: 20 min

Ingredients

- 2 ¾ cups all-purpose flour
- 5 tablespoons butter, divided
- 1 cup water
- 2 -(1/4 ounce each) active dry yeast
- 1/2 cup old-fashioned oats
- 1/4 cup honey
- 1 teaspoon salt
- 3/4 cup whole wheat flour
- 1 large egg, room temperature

Preparation

1. Mix one cup of all-purpose flour, oats, whole wheat flour, yeast, and salt in a large bowl. Heat water, honey, and 4 tablespoons of butter to 120°-130°C in a small saucepan. Add to dry ingredients and then beat on medium speed for 2 minutes. Add an egg and beat on high for 2 minutes. Stir in enough remaining all-purpose flour to form a soft dough (dough will be sticky).
2. Turn dough onto a floured surface; knead until smooth and elastic, about 6-8 minutes. Place in a greased bowl, turning once to grease the top. Cover with plastic wrap and let rise in a warm place until doubled, about 1 hour.
3. Punch it down, then turn it onto a lightly floured surface. Divide and shape the dough into 24 balls—place in a greased 13x9-inch baking pan.
4. Cover with a kitchen towel. Let rise for about 30 minutes in a warm place until it doubles,
5. Preheat oven to 375°. Bake 20-22 minutes or until golden brown. Melt remaining butter; brush over rolls. Remove from pan to a wire rack.

Nutrition Facts

Calories: 103

Fat: 3g

Cholesterol: 15mg

Sodium: 126mg

Carbohydrate: 17g

Protein: 3g

83. LEMON-RASPBERRY STREUSEL MUFFINS

Prep: 15 min

Baking: 20 min

Ingredients

- 2 cups all-purpose flour
- 1/2 cup sugar
- 2 teaspoons baking powder
- 1/2 teaspoon baking soda
- 1/2 teaspoon salt
- 2 large eggs, room temperature, lightly beaten
- 1 cup lemon yogurt
- 1/2 cup vegetable oil
- 1 teaspoon grated lemon zest
- 1 cup fresh or frozen raspberries

Topping

- 1/3 cup sugar
- 1/4 cup all-purpose flour
- 2 tablespoons butter or margarine

Preparation

1. Combine flour, baking powder, baking soda, sugar, and salt in a large bowl. Combine eggs, yogurt, oil, and lemon zest; mix well. Stir into dry ingredients just until moistened.
2. Fold in raspberries and fill greased or paper-lined muffin cups three-fourths full.
3. For the topping, combine sugar and flour. Cut in the butter until mixture resembles coarse crumbs; sprinkle about one tablespoon over each muffin.
4. Bake at 400°C for 18-20 minutes or until the muffins test is done.
5. Cool in pan for 10 minutes; remove from pan to a wire rack.

Nutrition Facts

Calories: 272

Fat: 12g

Cholesterol: 41mg

Sodium: 258mg

Carbohydrate: 37g

Protein: 4g

84. JAPANESE MILK BUNS

Prep time: 2 hours 50 minutes

Cook time 20 minutes

Total time 3 hours 10 minutes

Ingredients

Tangzhong

- 3 tablespoons water
- 3 tablespoons whole milk
- 2 tablespoon all-purpose flour

Bread dough

- 2 ½ cups all-purpose flour
- ½ cup whole milk warm (105 F)
- 1 tsp. salt
- 1/4 cup unsalted butter melted
- 2 tablespoon whole milk powder
- 1/4 cup sugar
- 1 tablespoon active dry yeast
- 1 tablespoon milk for brushing on the buns
- 1 large egg

Preparation

Tangzhong

1. Stir together milk, water, and flour until lump-free in a small pot. Cook it over low heat, keep stirring continuously until the mixture becomes thick, forming a paste. Transfer it to a small bowl and let cool.

Dough

2. Add the warm milk to a large mixing bowl, and then sprinkle the yeast and about one teaspoon of the sugar. Let the mixture for approximately 5 minutes to activate the yeast. Add the sugar, butter, egg, milk powder, salt, and cool tangzhong. With a big wooden spoon, incorporate all the ingredients. Add the flour and stir it into the rest of the mixture. Once the dough forms a shaggy mass, turn it to a surface sprinkled with flour.

3. Knead the dough until it is smooth, elastic, and soft.
4. Shape the dough into a ball and place it in a lightly greased bowl; cover the bowl and let it rise for about 90 minutes until puffy. Divide dough into nine portions, shape each into a ball, and place each on a greased 9-inch baking pan. Cover the rolls, and then let them rise for another 50 minutes.
5. Preheat oven to 350 F. Follow up with brushing the surface of the rolls with milk. Bake at 350F for approximately 17 minutes or until the tops are golden. Serve while warm. The leftovers are stored at room temperature for up to 2 days in a tightly covered container

Nutrition Facts

Calories: 231

Fat: 7g

Cholesterol: 37mg

Sodium: 282mg

Potassium: 104mg

Carbohydrates: 35g

Protein: 6g

Calcium: 46mg

85. OVERNIGHT CINNAMON ROLLS

Prep: 35 min

Baking: 20 min

Ingredients

- 2 - (1/4 ounce each) active dry yeast
- 1 ½ cups warm water (110° to 115°)
- 2 large eggs, room temperature
- 1/2 cup butter, softened
- 1/2 cup sugar
- 2 teaspoons salt
- 6 ¼ cups all-purpose flour

Cinnamon **filling**

- 1 cup packed brown sugar
- 4 teaspoons ground cinnamon

- 1/2 cup softened butter, divided

Glaze

- 2 cups confectioners' sugar
- 1/4 cup half-and-half cream
- 2 teaspoons vanilla extract

Preparation

1. In a small bowl, dissolve yeast in warm water. In a large bowl, combine eggs, butter, sugar, salt, yeast mixture, and 3 cups flour; beat on medium speed until smooth. Stir in enough remaining flour to form a very soft dough (dough will be sticky). Do not knead. Cover; refrigerate overnight.
2. In a small bowl, mix brown sugar and cinnamon. Turn dough onto a floured surface; divide dough in half. Roll 1 portion into an 18x12-inch rectangle. Spread with 1/4 cup butter to within 1/2 in. of edges; sprinkle evenly with half of the brown sugar mixture.
3. Roll up jelly-roll style, starting with a long side; pinch seam to seal. Cut into 12 slices. Place in a greased 13x9-inch baking pan, cut side down. Repeat with remaining dough and filling.
4. Cover with kitchen towels; let rise for about 1 hour in a warm place until it doubles—Preheat oven to 375°.
5. Bake for 20-25 minutes. Mix cream, confectioners' sugar, and vanilla; spread over warm rolls.

Nutrition Facts

Calories: 278

Fat: 9g

Cholesterol: 39mg

Sodium: 262mg

Carbohydrate: 47g

Protein: 4g.

86. SUPER SOFT CINNAMON ROLLS

Prep time: 20 mins

Cook time: 25 mins

Total time: 4 hours

Ingredients

Tangzhong starter

- 5 tablespoons water
- 5 tablespoons whole milk
- 10 teaspoons all-purpose flour

Roll dough

- 4 cups plus 2 tablespoons all-purpose flour
- 1¾ teaspoons salt
- 1 tablespoon instant yeast
- ¼ cup non-fat dry milk
- ¾ cup warm whole milk
- 2 large eggs, room temperature
- 6 tablespoons unsalted butter, melted

Filling

- 4 tablespoons unsalted butter, softened
- 1 cup lightly packed dark brown sugar
- 2 tablespoons ground cinnamon

Buttercream frosting

- 1 cup (2 sticks) unsalted butter, softened
- 3 cups sifted confectioners' sugar
- ½ teaspoon vanilla extract

Preparation

Making tangzhong starter

1. Combine the water, flour, and milk in a small saucepan over medium heat. Whisk together and cook, stirring, until the mixture thickens for 4 minutes. The combination will be the consistency of thick pudding. Remove it from heat and set it aside.

Dough

1. Combine the flour, instant yeast, salt, and dry milk in the bowl of an electric mixer fitted with the dough hook, add the warm milk, melted butter, eggs, and reserved tangzhong paste.
2. Mix the dough on medium speed until it combines to form a dry ball, and then cover the bowl with a clean towel. Let rest for about 20 minutes.
3. After 20 minutes, mix the dough on medium to high speed for two minutes until a smooth dough. Scrape down the dough from the dough hook as needed to blend evenly. Remove the dough hook, use a rubber scraper to bring the dough into a ball, and spray the cooking spray inside the bowl.
4. Transfer to a warm place in a covered bowl. Let it rise for about 60- 90 minutes until it almost doubles in bulk, depending on the warmth and environment. The finger imprint remains and does not bounce back when touched.

Filling

1. Turn the dough out and place it on a surface sprinkled with a bit of flour. Lightly press the dough into a small rectangular shape. Roll it into a 12-by-19-inch rectangle and spread the filling butter over the entire surface. Sprinkle it with brown sugar and cinnamon evenly over the top. Start with a long edge, rolling the dough around, filling it into a spiral log. Pinch the open edge so it stays together.
2. Use thread or a knife to cut the log into 15 rolls. Place the rolls cut side up in a buttered jelly roll pan and cover it. Let the rolls rise until they almost double in bulk, for 45-60 minutes, depending on the warmth and environment.

Baking

1. When rolls have been almost proofed thoroughly, heat oven to 350ºF with rack in the center, bake the rolls for 22-26 minutes until they turn golden.

Make buttercream

1. Beat the butter until smooth in a mixing bowl and add the confectioners' sugar a little at a time. Mix until the frosting comes together. Add vanilla and scrape down the sides of the bowl. Mix thoroughly.
2. Spread icing on warm, not hot, rolls.

Nutrition Facts

Calories: 479kcal

Carbohydrates: 67g

Protein: 6g

Fat: 21g

Cholesterol: 80mg

Sodium: 414mg

Fiber: 2g

Sugar: 40g

Calcium: 83mg

Iron: 2mg

87. BACON SCALLION MILK BREAD

Prep: 3 hours 35 minutes

Cook: 25 minutes

Total: 4 hours

Ingredients

- 1/4 cup cake flour
- 1/3 cup heavy cream
- 1/2 large egg, beaten
- 3 tablespoons sugar
- 1 ¾ cups bread flour
- 1 ½ teaspoon active dry yeast
- 1/2 cup whole milk
- ½ teaspoon salt
- 4 ounces bacon
- 1 cup scallions, chopped
- egg wash (1/2 egg with 1 teaspoon water)
- quick, simple syrup

Preparation

1. Take the heavy cream, milk, egg out of the refrigerator, and allow them to come up to room temperature, 30-45 minutes.

2. In the bowl of a stand mixer fitted with the dough hook attachment or a large mixing bowl, add the ingredients in the following order: heavy cream, milk, ½ of a beaten egg, sugar, cake flour, bread flour, yeast, and salt.
3. Turn the mixer to the lowest setting (or stir with a wooden spoon) and mix until a dough forms. Knead the dough on the lowest setting for 15 minutes, occasionally stopping the mixer from pushing the dough together. Extend the kneading by hand by about 5–10 minutes when kneading by hand.
4. When in a humid climate and the dough is sticking to the sides of the bowl, add a little more flour a tablespoon at a time. This is done until it pulls away from the sides. Don't add too much flour; this will make the bread denser and less fluffy.
5. Place in a warm spot and cover the bowl with a damp towel for 60-90 minutes to allow proofing until the dough doubles.
6. While proofing of the dough is complete, cook the bacon on both sides until crisp but pliable. Cool and chop into ½-inch pieces. Prepare the scallions by washing them thoroughly, drying, and finely chopping them. Grease a 9-inch round pan with butter thoroughly.
7. After the dough has risen, punch the air out of it. Knead for 5 minutes to form it into a round ball and roll it out into a ¼-inch thick rectangle. Sprinkle the scallions and the bacon evenly over the dough and cut it into small 1.5-inch squares.
8. Fold each into half like a taco with the bacon scallion filling inside. Nestle them in the cake pan standing up on one end of the taco. Meanwhile, cover and refrigerate the dough overnight. On the next day, remove the dough from the refrigerator, and let it come up to room temperature.
9. Proof the dough for an hour. Place a rack in the center of your oven and preheat it to 175°C and then brush the proofed dough top with egg wash and bake for approximately 25 minutes, or until they are golden brown in color.
10. Remove the bread from the baking oven and immediately brush with the sugar water mixture. This will give it a nice shine!
11. Cool, and enjoy while warm or at room temperature.

Nutrition Facts

Calories: 254kcal

Carbohydrates: 31g

Protein: 8g

Fat: 11g

Cholesterol: 40mg

Sodium: 259mg

Fiber: 2g

Sugar: 7g

Calcium: 39mg

88. ITALIAN SWEET BREAD

Prep: 10 min

Rising Bake: 20 min plus cooling

Ingredients

- 3 cups all-purpose flour
- 2 tablespoons butter, softened
- 1 cup warm 2% milk (70° C to 80°C)
- 2 teaspoons active dry yeast
- 1 teaspoon salt
- 1 large egg, lightly beaten
- 1/4 cup sugar
- Italian seasoning, optional

Egg wash

- 1 large egg
- 1 tablespoon water

Preparation

1. Place the first seven ingredients in the order suggested in the bread machine pan. Select dough setting and check the dough after 5 minutes after mixing. Add about two tablespoons of water or flour if necessary.
2. When the cycle is completed, turn dough onto a floured surface. Divide in half. Shape each portion into a ball; flatten slightly. Place in two greased 9-in. round baking pans. Cover and let rise until doubled, about 45 minutes.
3. Beat egg and water; brush over the dough. Sprinkle with Italian seasoning if desired. Bake at 350° until golden brown, 20-25 minutes. Remove from pans to wire racks to cool.

Nutrition Facts

Calories: 87

Fat 2g

Cholesterol: 22mg

Sodium: 119mg

Carbohydrate: 15g

Protein: 3g

89. EASY BANANA BREAD

Total time: 1 hour

Ingredients

- 1/3 cup shortening
- 1/2 cup sugar
- 2 eggs
- 1 ¾ cups all-purpose flour
- 1 teaspoon baking powder
- 1/2 teaspoon baking soda
- 1/2 teaspoon salt
- 1 cup mashed ripe bananas

Preparation

1. Mix cream shortening and sugar in a large bowl. Beat in eggs. Combine the flour, baking powder, baking soda, and salt; add to creamed mixture alternately with bananas, beating well after each addition. Pour into a greased 8x4-inch loaf pan.
2. Bake the dough for approximately 50 minutes at 350°C. Let stand for 10 minutes before removing from pan; cool on a wire rack.

Nutrition Facts

Calories: 133

Fat: 5g

Cholesterol: 27mg

Sodium: 146mg

Carbohydrate: 20g

Protein: 2g

90. CHALLAH BREAD

Preparation time 30 mins

Baking time: 35 mins

Rest time: 2 hours

Total time: 3 hours 5 mins

Ingredients

- ¼ cup sugar
- 1 package instant yeast
- 4 ½ cups all-purpose flour
- 3/4 cup of water
- 1/2 teaspoon salt
- ¼ cup vegetable oil
- 3 large eggs

Preparation

1. Combine flour, yeast sugar, and salt in a large mixing bowl. Add in vegetable oil, water, and two eggs and mix until well combined.
2. Using either a dough hook or a well-floured surface, knead for about 10 minutes. The dough will be smooth. Transfer to an oiled bowl and cover with plastic wrap. Let rise in a warm place for about 1 hour. It should have doubled in size.
3. After an hour, punch down the dough and let rise an additional 30 minutes.
4. Transfer dough to a lightly floured surface and divide into six evenly size pieces. Roll each piece into about 12-inch logs. Pinch the tops of all six strands together. Take the furthest right strand and cross it over the next two strands to the left. Weave the strand under the third and then back over the remaining two doughs.
5. Repeat the same procedure for the two; under one and over two for the remaining bread threads. Fold the remaining bread threads.
6. Transfer to a sheet pan, beat the remaining egg until smooth, and brush on the bread. Sprinkle poppy seeds or sesame seeds on top or leave it plain. Let rise for an additional 20–30 minutes.
7. Preheat the oven to 375F and bake for about 40 minutes.

Nutrition Facts

Calories: 758

Total Fat: 8g

Cholesterol: 47mg

Sodium: 110mg

Carbohydrates: 147g

Fiber: 5g

Protein: 21g

91. CHOCOLATE CHIP CRANBERRY BREAD

Prep: 20 min

Bake: 1 hour

Ingredients

- 2 cups all-purpose flour
- 3/4 cup sugar
- 2 teaspoons baking powder
- 1/2 teaspoon salt
- 1 large egg, room temperature
- 3/4 cup 2% milk
- 6 tablespoons butter, melted
- 1 cup fresh or frozen cranberries, halved
- 1 cup miniature semisweet chocolate chips

Streusel

- 1/3 cup packed brown sugar
- 2 tablespoons all-purpose flour
- 1/8 teaspoon ground cinnamon
- 2 tablespoons cold butter
- 3/4 cup confectioners' sugar
- 3 tablespoons whole milk

Preparation

1. Preheat the oven to 325°C and line the bottom of a greased 9x5-inch loaf pan with parchment.
2. Combine the flour, sugar, baking powder, and salt in a large bowl. Whisk butter, an egg, and milk; stir into dry ingredients until moistened. Fold in cranberries and chocolate chips. Transfer to prepared pan.
3. Combine flour, brown sugar, and cinnamon; cut in butter until crumbly in another bowl. Sprinkle over batter. Bake for 60-65 minutes.
4. Cool for 10 minutes; loosen sides of the bread from pan. Cool completely before removing from pan.
5. For the glaze, mix two tablespoons of milk and confectioners' sugar until smooth; if needed, add 1 tablespoon milk to reach the desired consistency. Drizzle glaze over top of bread; allow sitting 10-15 minutes before slicing.

Nutrition Facts

Calories: 253

Fat: 10g

Cholesterol: 28mg

Sodium: 193mg

Carbohydrate: 41g

Protein: 3g

92. CARROT ZUCCHINI BREAD

Prep: 10 min

Bake: 45 min

Ingredients

- 1 cup unsweetened applesauce
- 3/4 cup shredded carrots
- 3/4 cup shredded peeled zucchini
- 1/2 cup sugar
- 2 large eggs, room temperature
- 1 ½ teaspoons pumpkin pie spice
- 1 teaspoon ground cinnamon
- 1/2 teaspoon ground nutmeg
- 3 cups all-purpose flour
- 1 tablespoon baking powder
- 1/2 teaspoon baking soda
- 1/2 teaspoon salt
- 3/4 cup orange juice

Preparation

1. Combine the first 8 ingredients in a bowl or combine flour, baking powder, baking soda, and salt; add orange juice to carrot mixture
2. Pour them into 2 greased and floured 8x4-inch loaf pans.
3. Preheat oven to 350°C. Bake for about 45 minutes. Cool for about 10 minutes.

Nutrition Facts

Calories: 90

Fat: 1g

Cholesterol: 16mg

Sodium: 145mg

Carbohydrate: 19g

Protein: 2g

93. SWISS BEER BREAD

Prep: 15 min

Bake: 50 min

Ingredients

- 4 ounces Swiss cheese
- 3 cups all-purpose flour
- 3 tablespoons sugar
- 3 teaspoons baking powder
- 1 ½ teaspoons salt
- 1/2 teaspoon pepper
- 12 ounces beer or non-alcoholic beer
- 2 tablespoons butter, melted

Preparation

1. Preheat oven to 375°. Divide cheese in half. Cut half into 1/4-inch cubes; shred remaining cheese. Combine the next 5 ingredients in a large bowl. Stir beer into dry ingredients just until moistened. Fold in cubed and shredded cheese.
2. Transfer to a greased 8x4-inches loaf pan. Drizzle with butter. Bake for 50–60 minutes. Cool for 10 minutes; remove it from the pan and place it on a wire rack.

Nutrition Facts

Calories: 182

Fat: 5g

Cholesterol: 11mg

Sodium: 453mg

Carbohydrate: 28g

Protein: 6g

94. SPANISH SWEET MILK BREAD

Prep time: 90 mins

Cook time: 15 mins

Total time: 1 hour 45 minutes

Ingredients

- 500g bread flour
- 25g of baking powder
- 250 ml milk
- 70g melted butter
- 40g of sugar
- 1 large egg
- 2 tablespoon honey
- Pinch of salt

Preparation

1. Add the flour and baking powder to a large mixing bowl, and then add the egg and milk, honey, sugar, and salt. Mix. Add the melted butter and knead the dough for 12 minutes.
2. Form your dough into a ball and put it into a clean, floured mixing bowl; cover with a cloth and leave in a warm place for about two hours. Briefly knead again to remove any gas.
3. Separate the dough into hand-sized portions, form a rough cylinder, and roll flat to 1 cm thickness. Each piece should be in the shape of a rectangle using a sharp knife, making about 3 or 4 vertical cuts 1 cm apart and up to about a third of the length of the rectangle.
4. Roll up the dough starting with the uncut and just roll through the cuts. Ensure that the ends of the cuts are on the bottom of your rolls. This will keep them in check so that when you put them in the oven, they do not spread them open.
5. Preheat the oven to 200°C, and before putting the rolls in the oven, brush the surface of each with some milk. Sprinkle over some sugar—Cook for 15 minutes in a preheated oven.

95. VEGAN SODA BREAD

Prep time: 15 minutes

Cook time: 40 minutes

Total time: 55 minutes

Ingredients

- 3 cups all-purpose flour
- 1 cup white bread flour
- 1 teaspoon salt
- 1 teaspoon baking soda
- 1/4 cup coconut oil, melted

Vegan buttermilk

- 1 cup plant-based milk
- 1 tablespoon lemon juice

Preparation

1. Preheat the oven to 220°C and line a baking sheet with parchment paper.
2. Prepare the buttermilk (mix plant-based milk with lemon juice). Let it sit. Prepare the dry ingredients.

3. Combine baking soda, the flours, and salt in a large bowl; gradually stir in the melted coconut oil and buttermilk until the dough comes together in a slightly sticky ball.
4. Turn dough onto a floured surface. Knead a few times gently and form it into a ball and place it onto the baking sheet.
5. Cut an "X" into the dough (1/4 of an inch deep) with a sharp knife,
6. Bake for 35 minutes, remove the bread from the oven; transfer it to a wire rack; let it cool before slicing it.

Nutrition Facts

Calories: 193

Fat: 5g

Sodium: 313mg

Potassium: 44mg

Carbohydrates: 31g

Protein: 5g

Calcium: 31mg

96. VEGAN HOKKAIDO MILK BREAD

Prep time: 4 hours 20 minutes

Cook time: 45 minutes

Total time: 5 hours 5 minutes

Ingredients

Tangzhong

- 30g bread flour

- 85g water

- 85g soy milk

Dough

- 575g bread flour

- 7g active dry yeast

- 80g sugar

- 8g salt

- 25g water for emulsion

- 2 tsp. vanilla extract

- 200g soy milk (room temperature)

- 25g olive oil for emulsion

- 200g full fat coconut milk

Preparation

Tangzhong making

1. Combine the bread flour, milk, and water in a saucepan. Start to heat the mixture at medium heat and stir continuously until it thickens and to a paste.

2. Once ready, cover it with plastic wrap. Refrigerate it until you need it. Tangzhong can be made the day before.

Dough

3. Mix the soymilk with one teaspoon of the total sugar. Add the yeast and stir until everything dissolves.

4. Sift the flour and the salt in a separate bowl. When the yeast activates, add the sugar and the tangzhong and mix thoroughly. Add the coconut milk to the mixture and stir

5. Mix 25 ml of water with 25 ml of olive oil and stir until you get a whitish-yellowish viscous liquid. Add your wet ingredients to the flour and add the oil/water emulsion. Mix until there are no lumps of flour particles.

6. Let the dough rest 20-30 minutes to allow the flour to absorb moisture. Knead the dough until you can stretch it into a thin layer without tearing it apart. It should not be very sticky. Allow the dough to rest until it doubles in size.

7. Divide the dough into two halves of equal weight. For one part of the parts into four equal pieces, shape them into a small ball and let them rest for 5 minutes.

8. Take other pieces, flatten them with your hand into an oval, and stretch the oval into a larger one with a rolling pin. The narrow side should be as broad as the narrow side of your baking pan.

9. Roll the piece into a log and place it in a lightly oiled baking pan. Repeat for the other three pieces. Let rise for 1 hour until it is puffy

10. Preheat your oven at 340F. Bake the loaves until they brown in color.

Nutrition Facts

Calories: 105

Total Fat: 4g

Cholesterol: 9mg

Sodium: 313mg

Carbohydrates: 16g

Fiber: 1g

Sugar: 9g

Protein: 2g

97. GARLIC-DILL SODA BREAD

Prep: 15 min

Cook: 1 ½ hours

Ingredients

- 4 cups all-purpose flour
- 2 tablespoons dried parsley flakes
- 1 tablespoon dried minced onion
- 2 teaspoons garlic powder
- 1-1/2 teaspoons dill weed
- 1 teaspoon salt
- 1 teaspoon baking soda
- 1 teaspoon ground mustard
- 1-3/4 cups buttermilk
- 1 cup shredded sharp cheddar cheese

Preparation

1. Whisk the first eight ingredients in a large bowl and add cheese and buttermilk. Stir just until moistened. Turn onto a lightly floured surface. Knead gently about 8 times. Shape dough into a 6-inch round loaf and score the surface 1-inch deep with a sharp knife in a crisscross pattern. Place in a greased 5-qt. slow cooker.
2. Cook while covered, on high about 1 ½ hours
3. Preheat broiler. Remove bread; place on a baking sheet. Broil 6-8 inches from heat for 3 minutes. Allow it to cool on the wire rack completely.

Nutrition Facts

Calories: 209

Fat: 4g

Cholesterol: 11mg

Sodium: 434mg

Carbohydrate: 35g

Protein: 8g

98. VEGAN PUMPKIN BREAD

Prep: 10 min

Bake: 1 hour

Ingredients

- 3 ½ cups all-purpose flour

- 1 teaspoon ground cinnamon

- 1 teaspoon baking soda

- 2/3 cup water

- 1/2 teaspoon baking powder

- 3 cups sugar

- 15 ounces pumpkin

- 1 ½ teaspoons salt

- 1/2 teaspoon ground nutmeg

- 1 cup canola oil

- 2 teaspoons vanilla extract

Preparation

1. Whisk flour, sugar, salt, baking soda, cinnamon, nutmeg, and baking powder in a large bowl. Whisk pumpkin, oil, water, and vanilla in another bowl until it blends. Add to flour mixture, and then stir just until moistened.

2. Preheat oven to 350°C. Transfer to two greased 9x5-inch loaf pans lined with parchment. Bake for 50 minutes until a toothpick inserted in the center comes out clean.

3. Before removing the loaf from the wire racks, allow it to cool for 10 minutes.

Nutrition Facts

Calories: 190

Fat: 7g

Sodium: 159mg

Carbohydrate: 31g

Protein: 2g

99. ONION & GARLIC SODA BREAD

Prep: 20 min

Bake: 35 min

Ingredients

- 1 tablespoon olive oil
- 1 medium onion, chopped
- 5 garlic cloves, minced
- 4 cups all-purpose flour
- 1 teaspoon salt
- 1 teaspoon baking soda
- 1/4 cup cold butter, cubed
- 1 large egg, room temperature
- 1-1/2 cups buttermilk

Preparation

1. Preheat oven to 425°C., heat oil over medium-high heat in a small skillet. Add onion, then cook for 3-5 minutes and stir until light golden brown. Add garlic and cook while stirring for 30 seconds longer. Cool.
2. Whisk flour, salt, and baking soda in a large bowl; cut in butter until mixture resembles coarse crumbs. Stir in cooled onion mixture; make a well in the center. Whisk the buttermilk and an egg in a small bowl and pour into the well. Mix the dough until too stiff to stir with a wooden spoon. Turn onto a lightly floured surface. Knead gently about 10 times and shape into a round loaf.
3. Transfer into a large baking sheet; cut a shallow "X" on the top of the loaf with a sharp knife. Bake for 35-40 minutes.
4. Remove it from pan to a wire rack.
5. Serve warm.

Nutrition Facts

Calories: 219

Fat: 6g

Cholesterol: 27mg

Sodium: 398mg

Carbohydrate: 35g

Protein: 6g

100.   PANDAN HOKKAIDO MILK BREAD (VEGAN)

Prep time: 1 hour

Cook time: 45 minutes

Total time: 1 hour 45 minutes

Type: Vegan

Ingredients

Tangzhong

- 40g strong white bread flour

- 200 ml water

Milk bread

- 400g strong white bread flour

- 80g vegan butter room temperature

- 2 tbsp coconut milk powder

- 3/4 tsp. salt

- 80g caster sugar

- 2 tsp. pandan paste

- 2 tsp. instant yeast

- 125 ml full-fat coconut milk warmed to room temperature

For the vegan "egg wash"

- 2 tbsp agave

- 2 tbsp coconut milk

- 1/8 tsp. turmeric

Preparation

For tangzhong

1. In a small saucepan over medium heat of about 65°C/150°F, combine the flour and water and stir continuously for about 5 minutes or until the starter thickens to the consistency of mashed potato or a thick roux. Transfer it to a bowl and then cover it using a cling film. Allow it to sit until the starter gets to room temperature.

Dough

1. Add the sugar, coconut milk, and pandan paste to a saucepan and heat over low heat until the sugar has dissolved. Allow cooling at room temperature to about 38°C/100°F or just warm. Now add the yeast and stir. Set aside for 10 minutes until frothy.

2. Whisk coconut milk powder, bread flour, and salt in the stand mixer bowl. Once mixed, add tangzhong starter and warm milk. Whisk until it combines. Switch to the dough hook attachment and then knead the dough at medium-high speed for about 10 minutes.

3. With the mixer running, add the soft vegan butter one tablespoon until thoroughly combined; it will feel like much butter but keep it going. The butter is absorbed into the dough as it is kneaded. Turn the speed up to high and beat for a final 5 minutes. Transfer the dough to a lightly oiled bowl. Cover with cling film. Allow to sit for 60 minutes or until the dough has doubled in size.

Shaping the dough

1. Knock the air out of the risen dough and knead briefly to remove any large air pockets. Divide your dough into 14 equal parts. Keep the cut dough under cling film; this will prevent it from drying out or forming unwanted skin.

2. Take one portion of the dough and roll into a long oblong, about 5cm wide and 10cm in length. Roll it into a log starting from the end closest to you. Repeat with remaining dough.

3. Place the first seven logs seam-side up in a well-greased loaf tin (1800g/4lb) for the first and second layer; place the logs seam-side down. Cover the loaf tin with cling film. Allow it to rest in a warm place for 30 minutes until the dough has doubled volume.

4. Preheat the oven to 175°C

For the vegan "egg wash"

1. Combine all the ingredients for the vegan "egg wash." Gently brush on top of the risen dough.

2. Bake in the preheated oven until the top of the bread is a nice golden brown. If the bread top colors too quickly, place a foil tent over it to prevent burning.

3. Let the bread cool in the loaf pan for 5 minutes before unmolding while wearing oven gloves. The loaf should slip out easily once inverted. Allow the loaf to cool to room temperature on a wire rack.

Nutrition Facts

Calories: 230kcal

Carbohydrates: 30g

Protein: 6.6g

Fat: 9.4g

Saturated fat: 4.4g

Sodium: 228.9mg

Fiber: 1g

Sugar: 9.2g

101.   CLASSIC IRISH SODA BREAD

Prep: 15 min

Bake: 30 min

Ingredients

- 2 cups all-purpose flour
- 2 tablespoons brown sugar
- 1 teaspoon baking powder
- 1 teaspoon baking soda
- 1/2 teaspoon salt
- 3 tablespoons cold butter, cubed
- 2 large eggs, room temperature, divided use
- 3/4 cup buttermilk
- 1/3 cup raisins

Preparation

1. Preheat oven to 375°. Whisk together the first five ingredients. Cut in butter until mixture resembles coarse crumbs, whisk together one egg and buttermilk in another bowl. Add to flour mixture, then stir just until moistened. Stir in raisins.
2. Turn onto a lightly floured surface. Knead gently about 8 times. Shape into a 6 ½ -inch round loaf. Place on a greased baking sheet, then cut with a sharp knife to make a shallow cross on the top of the loaf. Whisk the remaining egg; brush over the top.
3. Bake for 30–35 minutes until golden brown. Remove from pan to a wire rack. Serve warm.

Nutrition Facts

Calories: 210

Fat: 6g

Cholesterol: 59mg

Sodium: 463mg

Carbohydrate: 33g

Protein: 6g.

102. IRISH SODA BREAD MUFFINS

Total time: 30 min

Ingredients

- 2 ¼ cups all-purpose flour
- 1/2 cup plus one tablespoon sugar, divided
- 2 teaspoons baking powder
- 1/2 teaspoon salt
- 1/4 teaspoon baking soda
- 1 teaspoon caraway seeds
- 1 large egg, room temperature
- 1 cup buttermilk
- 1/4 cup butter, melted
- 1/4 cup canola oil
- 3/4 cup dried currants or raisins

Preparation

1. Combine the flour, baking powder,1/2 cup sugar, baking soda, salt, and caraway seeds in a large bowl. Beat the egg, butter, buttermilk, and oil in another bowl. Stir into dry ingredients just until moistened. Fold in currants.
2. Fill greased muffin cups three-fourths full. Sprinkle with remaining sugar. Bake for 15 minutes at 400°C. Cool for 5 minutes before removing from pan to wire rack. Serve warm.

Nutrition Facts

Calories: 235

Fat: 9g

Cholesterol: 28mg

Sodium: 247mg

Carbohydrate: 35g

Protein: 4g

Congratulations on taking the first steps to learning something new. It is a fantastic journey towards the healthy life that you have chosen. The best milk bread recipes for a quick breakfast, snack, or dinner, among others, have been highlighted in this cookbook. With the availability of different varieties, one can easily bake their favorite soft and fluffy bread among the world's best-known cuisines in Japan, Italy, India, and China, resulting from the Yudane and tangzhong methods of milk-bread baking. Having a healthy choice will help you to avoid obesity, heart diseases, diabetes, hypertension, and others associated with the consumption of fast foods.

This cookbook contributes to healthy living with various recipes even for vegetarians and diabetic individuals in mind. It gives basic and simple recipes along with complex ones that any individual can afford and easily bake. The equipment needed for cooking, refrigeration, and the ingredients to use are also readily available. This book should not be used to undermine the advice of a dietitian on which foods to consume (or not consume), and you should plan your meals to control your eating. It is essential to establish alternatives from dietitians if, with time, there is an accumulation of nutrients such as potassium, phosphorus, and sodium. This will significantly reduce the pace at which lifestyle diseases manifest themselves. Therefore, living healthy and on a balanced diet will ensure that one has reduced encounters of disease, thus reducing the incidences of dialysis and kidney transplant in case of kidney diseases.

I hope that this cookbook will significantly contribute to your personal transformation toward living a healthy life. The top dietitians have vetted the knowledge provided, focusing on enhancing proper diet and fostering healthy living. Enjoy your bread and the best recipes from this moment onwards!

Made in the USA
Coppell, TX
17 July 2022

80101857R00083